DESTINY OR DELUSION

CONTRIBUTORS:

Leonard Beaton

Richard Body, M.P.

Lionel Gelber

The Rt. Hon. Lord Greenwood

Brian Griffiths

Sir John Hunter

The Rt. Hon. Douglas Jay, M.P.

Professor Harry Johnson

Professor Nicholas Kaldor

William Pickles

David Stephen

David Wall

DESTINY OR DELUSION:

BRITAIN AND THE COMMON MARKET

Edited and with an Introduction by
DOUGLAS EVANS

LONDON
VICTOR GOLLANCZ LTD
1971

ISBN 0 575 00701 X

MADE AND PRINTED IN GREAT BRITAIN BY
THE GARDEN CITY PRESS LIMITED
LETCHWORTH, HERTFORDSHIRE
SG6 1JS

CONTENTS

DESTINY OR DELUSION

INTRODUCTION

Should Britain join the EEC? The question has been framed and answered variously over the last decade. What is not yet fully appreciated by the general public (even by some of the leadership of Britain) is that on the answer to this question hinges not only the future of Britain and much of Europe, but also, as this book attempts to demonstrate, the pattern of world political and economic alignments for a very long time to come; in particular whether they will become regional or inter-continental in character. Far from being a debate about the price of butter this is a debate about whether it is in the best interests of Britain and the world community as a whole that Britain should join the EEC.

It should be made perfectly clear at the outset that this book represents the views of twelve completely independent contributors. If it expresses a prevailing tone of scepticism about the benefits likely to accrue from British entry, this is because they have taken a hard look at the facts. Some contributors believe that the Treaty of Rome, and the Community that has grown from it, simply cannot accommodate British interests, so that, whatever the terms, Britain should not enter. Others would withhold judgement until the precise terms are known. None of the contributors begins with a narrow nationalist view of Britain's future. All are in favour of the fullest British involvement with our Continental neighbours while expressing reservations about the form the Community has taken and the possibility of its being reconciled with Britain's fundamental interests. *The Times*, perhaps the foremost advocate amongst the Press of British entry, defined (in an entirely different context) Britain's fundamental interest in world affairs as twofold[1]: "The pursuit of national interests is rightly the first concern of this or any other British Government. They can be stated in broad permanent terms, such as the free flow of trade and the maintenance of a power balance in the world, and in Europe in particular." If one accepts this *Times* definition, the weight of the evidence surveyed in the second half of this book in particular would suggest that British entry into the EEC would further neither of these aims.

It is worth mentioning in passing that as the purely economic arguments for entry are advanced less and less by the advocates of entry, so the political reasons, probably the basic motivation for joining, are finally assuming a pre-eminent position in their advocacy. Far from being internationalist, many advocates of entry assume, or at the very least hope, that Britain will be able to bend the EEC to her political will. The belief that once in the Community France and Germany will cancel each other out leaving Britain as the dominant partner is becoming more and more apparent. Just as an enlarged EEC is meant to stand between the United States and the Soviet Union as a Third Force, so Britain is envisaged as a Third Force between France and Germany. The prospect that the EEC may develop into a tight federal unit is banished from the mind.

In all this the concept that Britain can once again become a world power of the first rank is unquestioningly assumed. The idea that in a world where the pattern of international relations, political and economic, changes with unprecedented rapidity, Britain has a middle-power role to play based upon influence born of her unique world-wide experience has been insufficiently explored. The truth is that Britain can never attain equality with the world's superpowers since she lacks the population, the economic strength and the military capacity upon which political power rests in the modern world. The idea that entry into the EEC will somehow change this basic fact is a dangerous fantasy. Even assuming the Ten achieved a viable political unity—which is a very big assumption—there is little to suggest that such a hybrid union would emerge as Britain writ large. Nor should it.

Meanwhile, it is now almost ten years, spanning two Conservative and one Labour Government, since Britain first made

[1] See *The Times*, leader, *Crisis without Benefit*, Wednesday, January 20th, 1971.

application to join the European Economic Community. Something of the continuity of that application is seen in the fact that the minister responsible for negotiations in 1962-63 is now Prime Minister. It can fairly be assumed that throughout this period the Whitehall Ministries responsible, notably the Commonwealth and Foreign Office, have loyally promoted, if not exceeded, their political masters' commitment to the EEC. Television, radio and Fleet Street, sharing a common factor of being highly centralised and subject to fashionable assumptions, have acted as a willing publicity vehicle for official Government policy. Yet in spite of all this effort on the part of politicians, civil servants, economists, industrialists and publicists (not excluding the EEC Information Centre in London which costs the Community an unspecified sum) it is the lack of public enthusiasm for the long-term as well as the short-term prospects that have been the great missing factor in the ten-year debate now reaching its climax. For the moment the majority of the British people remain either hostile or sceptical, or merely bored with the whole question of British entry.

One of the reasons for this has undoubtedly been either the unwillingness, or the inability, of the keenest advocates of entry to present a thoroughgoing case for the benefits which will accrue permanently from British membership. That a case for British membership exists is not in serious dispute. Equally, until the full terms are known no ultimate decision can be made on this historic question. Meanwhile, beyond the small print of the negotiating documents and the day-to-day debate in public and in private, what is seriously lacking is some sort of overall assessment within a disciplined framework of the issues involved. In the past altogether too many issues have been treated irresponsibly. This is emphasised by the fact that many of the contributors to this symposium have done considerable original research in fields where one would have thought it was essential for the Government of the day not only to know the facts themselves, but also to make them known to the public at large.

This book then is an attempt to examine in depth the nature of the short-term, but more especially the long-term, issues which face the British people at this time.

Douglas Evans
January 1971

PART ONE

The Immediate Issues

I

THE ECONOMIC BURDEN OF ENTRY

by the Rt. Hon. Douglas Jay, M.P.
former President of the Board of Trade

THE ECONOMIC BURDEN imposed upon Britain by entry
into the Common Market on the terms proposed by Mr Heath
and Mr Geoffrey Rippon would be so heavy as to be crippling to
us as a nation. The burden would take the form of an immense
and self-inflicted load on our standard of living and our livelihood. Moreover it would last for as long as the Common Market
conducted its food, agricultural and trading policies on their
present lines.

Quite apart from any statistics, the reason why this country
would suffer such huge losses is simple and clear. We import
about 20 per cent of our national income, including about half
our food and most of our raw materials. We pay for this by
exporting manufactured goods competitively all over the world.
Joining the Common Market in its present form means funda-
mentally that we would buy our food from dear sources instead
of cheap; that we would raise our export costs over the whole of
British industry; that we would lose preference and free entry
rights for our exports in a far larger area of the world than that
in which we should gain; and that we would have to pay a huge
sum out of our own budget revenue across the exchanges to the
Common Market authorities. Any country, at any time, or in any
area, whatever the figures, which imports 20 per cent of its
national income must—should it decide to raise its import prices
gratuitously, sacrifice export privileges over much of the world,
assume, also gratuitously, huge "reparation" payments and in-
cidentally abandon control of capital exports—suffer huge and
lasting economic losses as a result. This is bound to be true, whatever the precise arrangements, "transitional" periods, or financial
calculations.

The loss is a basic economic one, in terms of trading ratios and therefore living standards. What would happen, essentially, would be this. We would put ourselves needlessly in a position where the British people would have to manufacture and sell abroad more motor cars to secure the same amount of wheat and feeding stuffs, more machine tools to buy the same amount of beef and mutton, more ships to buy the same butter and cheese, and more chemicals to buy the same volume of oil, rubber, metals, cotton and wool. This would mean, in plain English, that every British worker would have to work longer in return for the same real standard of living he might have had if we had not joined; or alternatively he would have to accept a lower real return for the same work as before. This is, of course, what a lower standard of living means. At the same time the burden would be made still greater by the fact that our exports would be less competitive thanks to higher costs, and that we would have to export a wholly additional and major slice of exports in order to finance the tribute or "levy" payment. On top of all that, the loss of export privileges throughout EFTA and the Commonwealth area would make exporting more difficult, and therefore the effort required for a given total of sales even greater.

All this would be true, not just for man-made avoidable arrangements due to mistaken policies, but also because we should be deciding to buy our main imports from areas ill-suited to produce them, instead of from the parts of the world where for geographical and climatic reasons costs are low. Any country's standard of living is highest if it buys its imports from those producers anywhere in the world who have the lowest costs. It so happens that Britain imports very large amounts of grain and feeding stuffs, meat, dairy produce, sugar and other foods. It also happens that, for basic physical reasons, butter and cheese are produced more cheaply in New Zealand than anywhere else in the world; mutton and lamb in Australia and New Zealand; wheat and feeding stuffs in Canada, Australia and the United States; and sugar in tropical areas of the Caribbean and in the Indian Ocean—all more cheaply than they can be in Europe. All this is due to geography, and not just to the inefficiency of farmers on the Continent, though in fact such needless inefficiency has made the gap even wider than it need have been. If, therefore, Britain chooses to buy large and essential imports from high-cost areas rather than low-cost areas, our standard of living must as a result be reduced permanently below what it might have been, whatever detailed devices are adopted to soften or conceal the blow.

The basic fall in living standards, which is inevitable, may show itself in one of three ways. But show itself it must. First, if the inevitable rise in retail prices of essential goods is not accompanied by rising money wages and salaries, it will show itself straightforwardly as a fall in real living standards due to higher prices combined with the same money incomes. Secondly, if money wages and salaries are raised to offset the higher prices, imports of consumer goods will rise and exports will be held back by higher costs. The national loss will then show itself in the form of a growing balance-of-payments deficit, which the Government must combat either by cutting back incomes directly, or by devaluation of the currency. Devaluation, thirdly, does not of course conjure away by a magic wand the fall in living standards. It merely converts it from a balance-of-payments deficit into a lower national real income, caused by the fact that prices of imports rise and that exports have to be sold at lower prices in foreign currency—in other words, we have to make and sell more cars in order to buy the same amount of wheat and meat. Devaluation, therefore, though it might well prove necessary, would not magically eliminate the economic burden. It would merely transmute it into another form. To suppose that it can do otherwise is a mere confusion of thought.

For another reason, before any statistical calculations are made, it is clear that there must be a net economic loss to Britain. The total consequences can be considered as, on the one hand, those affecting trade and exchanges between Britain and the Common Market, and secondly those affecting our trade and exchanges with the whole of the rest of the world. Look first at the balance of trade with the Common Market itself. Tariffs on industrial goods will go down to zero on both sides, but our labour costs will rise as a result of the change, and those of the present Common Market countries will not. Therefore, imports into Britain from the Six are bound to increase faster than our exports to the Six. This would be true even if our industrial tariffs were level on average with the external industrial tariff of the Six. But since in fact they are rather higher, the net balance of trade would move even further against us.

Look secondly at the consequences in the non-EEC world.

Every single consequence is adverse. We lose free entry rights and preference throughout the whole Commonwealth Preference Area, and much of EFTA. Our export costs go up, and others' do not. Our manufactured imports increase, because of our rise in costs. Therefore, since we lose on balance in exchanges with the Six, and since every consequence is a loss in the rest of the world, clearly—again before any figures are even estimated—we must inevitably suffer a major worsening of our trade balance with the world as a whole.

There are some who wishfully ask : If this is the undeniable cost of entering the Common Market on the terms proposed, is there not some "cost of staying out" to set off against it? To ask this is crudely to misunderstand the logic of the argument. The above economic argument, and the figures that follow, describe the difference between the situation of Britain if we do join the EEC, and if we do not. The cost of entry is precisely the same thing as the advantage of staying out. There is no additional "cost of staying out", and to suppose so is just another simple confusion.

It is no surprise, therefore, that the figures show what they must show. But their value is to demonstrate how great the loss must be in relation to the total trade and resources of Britain. The total burden on the balance of payments would be made up of the following main separate burdens or losses : (1) The extra price of food imports bought from high-cost, inefficient producers overseas instead of from low-cost efficient ones; (2) The "levy" or tribute payments to the Brussels agricultural funds designed to bolster up antiquated agriculture on the Continent and subsidise the huge bureaucracy in Brussels; (3) The loss of British exports due to the complete loss of free entry and preference rights in the Commonwealth Preference Area and their partial loss in EFTA; (4) The loss of exports all over the world due to higher British labour costs; (5) The higher level of imported manufactured goods into this country from the outside world as well as the EEC due to our higher labour costs; (6) The movement of the balance of trade against us with the Common Market Six themselves for the reasons given above; and (7) The burden on the balance-of-payments capital account due to loss of exchange control over all funds exported to the enlarged Common Market.

First would be the rise in the price of food imports. This would take two forms, one of which is often forgotten. One would be the obvious fact that we would to a major extent buy dear food from the Continent instead of far cheaper food from the outside world. In many cases, such as dairy produce and sugar, this would involve a price as much as double what we should otherwise have to pay. The other would be the need to pay very much higher prices—certainly often double again—for the food we now buy from the Common Market itself to the not negligible total of about £200 million a year. It is one of the ironies of entry that, whereas we now have the advantage of buying this Common Market food at the dumped price which the Six sell their surplus products abroad, we should if we joined enjoy the blessing of having to pay the prices (two or three times as high) which the Brussels authorities inflict on their own imprisoned consumers. Not merely food, of course, but feeding-stuff imports—one major cost of British agriculture—would also be much dearer. Since our total food and feeding-stuff imports are now over £2,000 million a year, it is clear that the increased burden on the balance of payments from higher food and feeding-stuff import prices must be at least £250 million a year, in 1971-72 prices.

The next instalment of the burden would be the tribute or "contribution" to the Brussels agricultural relief funds. This would in effect represent an entirely needless tax on the British consumer in order to finance antiquated and inefficient agriculture on the Continent, and to subsidise tax evasion by the wealthier taxpayers in France and Italy. It would amount in effect to subsidising tax evasion, because if the collection of direct taxes in France and Italy were at least as honest and efficient as it is at present in Britain, the agriculture of those countries could be financed from their own tax revenues without having to call for blood transfusions from the British taxpayer.

To finance these annual tribute payments, 90 per cent of the new food taxes and of our Customs revenue, and a slice of Purchase Tax or VAT revenue would have to be handed over each year as soon as the Common Market system was in full swing. The White Paper issued by the then Labour Government in February 1970 showed that these budget payments alone could be as high as £670 million a year. Mr Rippon, in a memorandum presented to the Brussels Commission in July 1970, estimated them at £468 million a year, if no major concessions were made in the course of negotiations. There seems no evidence that concessions which have been made, which are entirely trivial, would reduce the net figure below about £400 million a year.

The total extra burden, therefore, from the first two items— higher food prices and tribute payments—would be unlikely to be less than about £650 million a year on the import side of the balance, and *most unlikely to be less than £600 million*. This represents what may be called *the direct food and agricultural cost to Britain of joining the EEC*.

Thirdly would be the loss of British exports due to the raising of tariffs against us throughout a large part of the world. Tariffs would be raised against British goods throughout the whole of the Commonwealth Preference Area and that part of EFTA which did not join the EEC. Nearly 30 per cent of British exports are sold in the Commonwealth Preference Area—which includes Ireland, Burma and South Africa, as well as the Commonwealth itself—and another 15 per cent of our exports go to EFTA. A total of 45 per cent of our exports are thus sold in the Commonwealth and EFTA together, compared with 20 per cent in the Common Market. These percentages have not changed much in the last few years, after readjusting themselves to the post-war world, and are not likely to change much further in future if we avoid entanglement with the Common Market. If we do join, however, and erect reverse preferences and insuperable import barriers on food products against the Preference Area countries, these countries will inevitably cancel the free entry and preference which they now give to our goods, and impose on them the same m.f.n. duties as they now apply to exports from say Japan, the United States and the Common Market.

In those EFTA countries which did not join the Common Market—probably Sweden, Finland, Austria, Switzerland and Portugal—British exports would lose both the complete free entry they now enjoy, and their present preference over exports from the Common Market and all other countries. In those EFTA countries which perhaps did join, Denmark and Norway, we should retain free entry, but lose the preference we now enjoy as compared with the Six.

Thus British exports would suffer big losses in both the preference area and EFTA. In the Preference Area our biggest losses would be in Australia, Canada, South Africa and New Zealand. Canada, Australia and South Africa are all among our eight biggest export markets in the world, and Sweden and Switzerland are also highly important. Total British exports to the Preference Area and the EFTA countries not likely to join the EEC, are now nearly £2,500 million a year. To the four Preference Area countries that really matter—Canada, Australia, New Zealand and South Africa—our exports are already over £1,000 million. In these countries, 60 per cent of our exports enter duty-free and a higher proportion with a preference. If these privileges were cancelled, and the normal m.f.n. tariff imposed against us, it is clear that our exports would fall massively below the figure they would otherwise have reached. To these four countries the fall would be bound to be something of the order of £150-£200 million, and could not be less than £200 million for the Preference Area as a whole.

This estimate is strikingly confirmed by the C.B.I.'s inquiry into the consequences of joining the EEC (pages 58-59), which shows that the loss of exports in the Preference Area alone would just about equal the gain in the EEC, as a result purely of tariff changes in each case. This conclusion is highly important for many other reasons; but it reinforces the conclusion that exports of about £200 million a year would be lost in the Preference Area, since this is a reasonable estimate of what might be gained in the EEC.

In addition to this, however, Britain would lose exports both in that part of EFTA not joining the EEC, because tariffs would be raised against us, and also to some extent in those which do join, since we should lose our preference there against the Six. The British motor car industry for instance would lose materially in Switzerland and Sweden, whether they join the new group or not. Probably the loss of exports in EFTA could not be put at less than £50 million at the minimum; so that the total loss due to tariff changes would be at least £250 million, or already more than the gain in the Common Market.

Some have tried to argue that the loss in the Preference Area would not be as large as this, because the share of our exports going to the Preference Area and EFTA in the future would have fallen anyway. This is largely a misunderstanding of the argument, because the above calculation measures the *effect of the tariff changes, whatever would have happened without them.* But in addition to this, there is no reason to think that the share of our trade which is conducted with the Preference Area and EFTA would decline in the future if we did not join the Six.

British exports to the Commonwealth have increased nearly tenfold in value since 1938 and have doubled in volume. In recent years they have been increasing particularly fast. Between 1966 and 1969, our total exports to the Preference Area rose from £1,770 million to £2,217 million, and our imports from the Preference Area rose from £2,026 million to £2,530 million. During the period between 1938 and 1950, the share of our trade conducted with the Preference Area greatly increased, because the war stopped trade with many other countries; and since the 1950s, it has naturally reverted to normal. There is no reason to expect much change in the future, if we retain our import privileges particularly into Australia, Canada and South Africa, which are very large and very rapidly growing markets. Australia, indeed, as the *Economist* has said, has the potentiality of a second United States.

So much for the loss of British exports due to tariff changes if we joined the EEC. This, however, would only be the beginning. We should, fourthly, be faced with an additional heavy loss all over the world outside the Six due to higher labour costs. The rise in British living costs caused by the higher Common Market food prices was estimated by the Government's White Paper of February 1970 as 4-5 per cent, without allowing for Value Added Tax. The C.B.I. believed that VAT would add another 1.5-2 per cent. In addition to this, the higher social security contributions imposed on employers would enforce some further rise on the level of prices generally; so that it would be prudent to assume that British living costs would be permanently 7 per cent higher than they would have been, and that labour costs would be correspondingly higher also. Recent experience, and recent studies of elasticity of demand, suggest that this would mean a drop in the total value of British exports by about 6 per cent compared with what would have been achieved if we had not joined. Since our total exports outside the EEC now total about £6,000 million a year, it is inevitable that we should lose an additional £300 million a year of exports outside the EEC, due to higher labour costs. *This means a total loss of exports outside the Six of about £550 million a year.*

Fifth, the rise in British labour costs would of course affect not merely the competitive power of British exports, but British industry's competitiveness against manufactured imports in the home market. Japanese and American manufactured imports would tend to increase because our costs of production had risen and theirs had not. Textile imports, for instance, would be bound to increase for this reason. To set off against this, there would doubtless be some drop in British manufactured imports from EFTA countries which lost their free market here and from Commonwealth countries also. But these savings would be small, since a very low proportion of our imports from the Commonwealth are manufactured goods. On balance, I have little doubt that the increase in manufactured imports from the outside world would exceed the saving from the Commonwealth and EFTA. But one may perhaps optimistically assume that the difference would be small; and that though the trade balance would move further against us for that reason, this loss may be hopefully left out of the calculation.

Sixth, what is certain, however, is that Britain's trade balance with the Six itself would in addition worsen seriously. The Six would gain two advantages in exporting to us, as was pointed out above. Our tariffs would go down to zero; and our costs would rise, while theirs would not. But we, in exporting to them, would enjoy one advantage set off by one major disadvantage. Their tariffs would fall; but our costs would rise. Since our post-Kennedy industrial tariff would be rather higher than theirs, we must suffer relatively even more than them from the change. In the case of motor cars, for instance, anybody with the slightest knowledge of industrial facts must acknowledge that higher imports here from Germany and Italy would vastly exceed our higher exports in return. Since we have already seen, consistently with the C.B.I.'s estimates, that our total gain in exports to the Six might be about £200 million a year, it appears inevitable that our trade balance with the Six would worsen by £50-£100 million. *The total loss on the visible trade balance in non-food products, therefore, appears likely to equal £600-£650 million a year net from all quarters* (after having allowed for the gain in exports to the EEC).

Even this, however, is not the end of the burden on Britain's balance-of-payments. So far only the current account has been considered. But on top of all this, we should be compelled by the Treaty of Rome itself, which lays this down in indisputable black and white, to remove all exchange control on exports of British funds to the other members of the larger group. Since this has not been permitted at any time since 1939, few realise what an enormous further drain it might involve. Yet, if this were proposed for any purpose other than joining the Common Market, it would be denounced as disastrous for the British economy. It is likely to cost a good deal more, for instance, than the East of Suez defence policy, which has so often been deplored as something we cannot afford. Capital exports naturally vary from year to year. But if sterling were weakened by the sort of current account deficit described above, refugee funds might very soon be running at several hundred million a year. If a serious estimate is therefore to be made of the genuine balance-of-payments burden, it would be most imprudent to allow less than an annual average of £200 million for extra capital exports.

Thus the overall burden of the balance of payments would be likely to comprise about £600 million from direct food and agricultural costs, £600-£650 million from the net worsening of visible trade in non-food products, and £200 million from the capital account; or a total of between £1,250 and £1,500 million a year in all. So many disingenuous attempts have been made, for doctrinal reasons, to scale the figures down, that some people may still be surprised to find them so high. But in fact the above estimates are made conservatively at each point, and the total burden could very well be much higher. To put it at less than £1,000 million in 1971-72 values would in my judgement be completely irresponsible and contrary to the evidence. Ever since 1945 we have all tended to *under-estimate* the balance-of-payments burden resulting from various proposed policies.

The balance-of-payments burden imposed on Britain as a result of joining the EEC would be permanent and not temporary. When the full burden had been assumed, we should be that much worse off indefinitely, for as long as the Common Agricultural Policy remained in force, as compared with our situation if we had not joined. After the full burden had been assumed, it would grow year by year in proportion to the growth in the volume and value of our total trade, though the proportion it bore to that trade need not itself grow further. The figures quoted above are in 1971-72 trade and money values, but with the full Common Market system assumed to be applied to Britain. This is probably the most illuminating way to make the calculation; though by the time the full system had come into force, trade volumes and prices would have risen a good deal further, and the actual total sterling values of the burden would be much greater than those quoted above.

It is thus misleading to describe the burden as an "impact" effect. It is only an impact effect in the sense that it begins at once, not in the sense that it ceases at any time thereafter. The existence of a so-called "transition" period, over which the burden is assumed, makes no difference to the reality of the burden. It no more matters whether it is incurred in four years, five years or six, than it would matter whether one went blind in four, five or six days. In either case, one would be equally crippled thereafter. The "transition" has no importance, except as a device to conceal from the British public what is really being done.

The most immediate and obvious effect of the payments burden, as already explained, would be the fall in living standards necessary to absorb it. If Britain were free to alter its exchange rate, this correction of the deficit and fall in standards could be achieved without an actual check to economic growth in this country. But the consequence of joining the EEC would be much more serious than that. Changes in exchange rate are to be banned from an early stage between members, and a Common Currency has already been adopted as the aim by 1980. Nor would it even be in Britain's power to enforce, in our interests, a change in exchange rates between the Common Market as a whole and the rest of the world. *In these circumstances, the balance of payments deficit would enforce internal squeeze policies, which would inevitably bring economic growth near to a halt in Britain.* There would be no alternative. This would be likely to be fully as damaging a consequence as the balance-of-payments burden itself. The secondary lasting consequences would be as serious as the primary and equally lasting ones. In such circumstances, the only prudent expectation must be that economic growth in Britain would fall even lower. What this means can be illustrated by the simple calculation that if Britain had joined the Common Market in 1961, and growth had been held down as a result to a 1 per cent rise per year in real GNP, our real national income today would be about 20 per cent lower than it is, and wages on average would be £5 a week less.

A further crucial conclusion follows from the above calculation of the effect of entry on Britain's visible trade. The total market for British industry in the long-term would be seriously narrowed as a result of entry. This follows from the fact that the loss of exports in the world outside the EEC would be greater than the gain of exports in the EEC, and that the latter gain would certainly be exceeded by the growth of manufactured imports into the British market both from the EEC and from elsewhere. That conclusion is implied in the C.B.I. calculation already quoted that the loss of exports to the Preference Area alone would equal the gain in the EEC, with a consequent net loss of exports in the world as a whole; and the same conclusion equally follows from the table given in paragraph 59 of the White Paper of February 1970, which shows a net worsening of Britain's visible non-food trade balance. Though these conclusions are beyond question, there are still people—some who should know better—who go on talking of a "wider market" if Britain joined the EEC. This is a simple fallacy. The market would not be wider. Because of the net loss of exports, and excess of imports as compared with the situation if Britain remained outside, the market would certainly be *narrower* indefinitely thereafter. Therefore, the alleged secondary effect of a narrower market—loss of economies of scale, lesser productivity and so forth—would additionally and steadily work against us, and aggravate the long-term damage still further.

Some half-hearted attempts have been made to argue that all the consequences described above might not occur, because either food prices in the world outside the EEC would rise towards EEC levels, and narrow the gap; or else because something on the lines of Dr Mansholt's plan for agricultural reform in the EEC would be adopted. These pious hopes are totally unconvincing. First, it was frequently argued in 1966 and 1967 that, owing to world grain shortages, world prices would rise nearer to EEC levels. Just the reverse happened. The whole long-term world prospect has now been radically altered by the so-called "green revolution", which has banished the spectre of rice and wheat shortage from the world for as far ahead as can be foreseen. New strains of wheat and rice have enormously raised productivity in Asia; and though it takes time for these to spread to all suitable areas, the process has moved remarkably rapidly in the last five years. Deficit countries in Asia have already become net grain exporters, and the probability is that this dramatic change in the world food outlook will now gain ground steadily. The temporary rise in world grain prices in 1970 was due to one year's failure in the American maize crop, which is not likely to occur again, except very infrequently. A sober estimate, therefore, makes it much more likely that the gap between world food prices—which are largely based on wheat, rice and feeding stuffs—and EEC prices will in future be wider rather than narrower; and that therefore the advantage to Britain of staying out will grow as the years go by.

Secondly, the idea that all would be set right by the magical device of Dr Mansholt's plan is likely to remain as great an illusion in the future as in the past. Dr Mansholt's plan has remained for years on paper, and is likely to stay there. Prices of food have never been substantially reduced in the EEC, though they frequently go up. Their level is determined not by the paper plan of learned bureaucrats, but by the deep political forces of agricultural protectionism, on which the majority parties in France, Germany and Italy depend for their strength. These are no more likely to weaken in the next generation than they have in the past three or four. There is no political force in the world so stubborn as a vested interest in agricultural protection. It took the Irish potato famine to break it in Britain; and anyone who stakes our national fortunes now on this miracle being repeated in the EEC is being frivolous and irresponsible. But if, *per impossible*, this miracle were performed, the time for Britain to join would be *after* and not before it had become an accomplished fact. We should believe it when we see it. There is no reason whatever why this country should pay for a painful transmutation of others' obsolete policies which we abandoned 130 years ago. Nor is there any hope that we could get these policies altered from within—since on the issue crucial to us, we should be in a minority of one.

When all these inescapable consequences for Britain have been made plain, last-ditch apologists for entry have been forced back on the argument that the EEC has discovered some magic secret of growth, which Britain could contract merely by joining; and that there are some mysterious and invisible "dynamic" advantages to be gained somewhere in the distance, lurking behind the all-too-solid, certain and immediate losses. But it is economic nonsense, first, to suppose that because some other country has shown greater growth than one's own, one can automatically achieve that growth by forming a Customs Union with it. The effect of forming such an economic alliance depends on the circumstances of the individual case, which in the instance of Britain joining the EEC have been analysed above. And the plain fact is that the balance-of-payments deficit would slow down growth even further. But even if this mystical argument were true, it would establish a case for Britain joining in a Customs Union or free trade area with almost any country in the world, starting with Japan, rather than the EEC. For *the outstanding fact is that the EEC's growth has slowed down since the Rome Treaty was signed,* and that since that time the growth of all OECD countries other than the EEC, and of EFTA countries other than Britain, have quickened. Clearly the Rome Treaty has had little to do with growth one way or the other. If the growth argument were relevant to this choice, it would establish a case for Britain remaining a member of EFTA.

This conclusion is reinforced by the report of the National Institute of Economic and Social Research of November 1970 on the alleged "dynamic" consequences of joining the EEC. It shows indisputably that these do not exist. The National Institute report establishes beyond doubt that growth in the EEC slowed down after the Rome Treaty was signed, whereas in most OECD and EFTA countries, it speeded up. It also shows that EEC countries have suffered a drop in their share of exports to the outside world since 1960, which balances the increase within the EEC ring-fence. The following conclusion of the National Institute really puts the matter beyond doubt : "It is hard to think that if the dynamic properties of a widening market were really as great as is sometimes suggested, the statistical evidence of their influence would be so completely and consistently lacking. . . . To accept a heavy burden of 'impact effects' as the price of entry, in the belief that the 'dynamic effects' are likely to be even bigger, would under these circumstances represent a triumph of hope over experience."

So much for the major balance-of-payments and national economic consequences of entry. These would be the most serious : and the whole nation would be weakened economically and therefore politically as a result. But to avoid false optimism, some other economic consequences must be briefly mentioned which are not the main theme of this chapter. First, a new burden of the order of £1,000 million or more on our balance-of-payments must weaken disastrously this country's capacity to give aid to developing countries. When balance-of-payments deficits are heavy, aid inevitably is the first item to be cut—particularly if exchange rates can no longer be altered.

Two other deplorable internal consequences would follow. First, the shift in the tax burden from direct taxation to food taxes, a VAT and much heavier insurance contributions, would redistribute national income backwards in Britain from the poor to the rich. Some contamination from the flagrant tax evasion in collection of direct tax revenue in France and Italy would probably spread to this country. As a result of these tax changes, much if not all the progress made in the last fifty years in Britain in achieving greater equality of income, which is the greatest single foundation of democratic stability, would be lost. We should risk moving back towards the sort of inequality prevailing in Italy and France, and the widespread support for extremist parties which this always provokes.

Secondly, the whole location-of-industry policy, which has gone far to eradicate the old depressed areas in Britain since 1945, would have to be reversed. It is suggested sometimes that a so-called "regional policy" would be adopted within the enlarged EEC. But this policy as understood in the EEC has little reality, because it is merely supported by largely ineffective Government grants and not by any direct controls. The reality of British location policy is the Industrial Development Certificate, which enables the British Government to refuse a firm a certificate for building a factory in the Midlands or the South-east and to grant it for one in Scotland, Wales, the North-east or Northern Ireland. But abolish exchange control on the export of capital to the Continent, as we should have to on signing the Rome Treaty, and any firm could defy the I.D.C. system by threatening to build its factory in Belgium or Holland. The whole natural centripetal force for industrial development in the enlarged EEC would be towards Belgium, Holland and the Lower Rhine area—the Midlands of the new group—and away from the British Isles. If at the same time, the I.D.C. system was undermined, as it would be, and control of policy taken out of British hands, the outlook for Scotland, Wales and the North of England and Northern Ireland would be disastrous. Immense forces would be working against them, and no British Government would have the power to mobilise counter-forces. The industrial decline in these areas would be made still worse by the fact that the Common Agricultural Policy, quite apart from national losses, would discriminate in favour of the South East of England and against the cattle and sheep farmers of the North and West. For grain and feeding stuffs prices would rise steeply, to the advantage of South and East England, at the cost of the North and West. On any rational expectation, the North and West, as a result of these cumulative forces, would face conditions of depression similar to those of the 1930s, if not worse.

This chapter is not concerned with the political consequences of British entry. But no one should ignore the inescapable fact that the grave economic weaknesses, which combined balance-of-payments deficit and slow growth must cause, would ever more grievously undermine our political strength year by year. In the world of the future, a country's political and military strength will depend on a strong balance-of-payments and steady industrial growth. To throw away both of these, and at the same time to alienate politically our best friends in the world by excluding their goods—notably Australia, New Zealand, Canada and the EFTA countries—would be a straightforward recipe for political decline.

To sacrifice economic gains for the sake of national independence may be a worthy national aim. To sacrifice some sovereignty for the sake of economic advantage might perhaps occasionally be justified. But to pay a huge price in order to give away a nation's political freedom and independence at the same time would seem to border—to put it mildly—on wilful suicide.

THE AGRICULTURAL ISSUES

by Richard Body, M.P.

Farmer and Secretary of the Conservative Parliamentary Trade Committee: Chairman of the Open Seas Forum: Vice-Chairman of the Conservative Parliamentary Committee on Horticulture.

"Agriculture need cause Britain no difficulty in joining: we are getting interested in your system of deficiency payments and you are getting interested in our import levies— so we can meet somewhere in the middle."

M. JEAN REY

THESE ENTHUSIASTIC WORDS concluded my interview with M. Rey four years ago, at a time when he was the President of the European Commission and was still an ardent advocate of our entry into the EEC. That was four years ago; the EEC was ready to be flexible and even accommodating. What has caused the hardening of their attitude and their desperate desire not to compromise their Common Agricultural Policy? Why did Mr Anthony Barber begin the negotiations by declaring, in the name of the British people, his acceptance of its present form?

The Treaty of Rome does not demand the petrification of any one particular kind of agricultural policy. The door is open to any system of support or even to none at all. Three of the commodities of lesser importance are indeed supported by deficiency payments, and Dr Sicco Mansholt, the EEC's Vice-President responsible for agriculture, has said[1] that an enlarged Community might adopt this system for mutton and lamb. The

[1] At a meeting of the Council of Ministers, Brussels, September 28th, 1970.

chosen policy, whatever it is, can be changed, provided that one essential condition is fulfilled, and that is that at any one time each member-country must subscribe to that same policy. The reason is plain enough. If an economic community—which is a term that implies a unified economy—is to be created, one cannot keep out the one factor that is the most dominant in the economy of all its members.

It has always been open to us to propose, as a condition of our entry, or at least as a subject for negotiation, a radical change in the Common Agricultural Policy. For two reasons we decided not to do so. In the first place, France has made it clear that she will not agree to any such change, and an applicant country that does not accept the present policy will receive her veto. That applies not only to the method of support but also to the scale of support, a matter of enormous importance to the taxpayers of Britain.

The other reason is that France has a philosophical view about agriculture which is quite different to our own. M. Jules Méline may have died decades ago, but Mélinism lives on as heartily as ever. An understanding of what it means is basic to any discussion about the Common Agricultural Policy. The peasants of France must be protected because they are her backbone; and when trouble comes from within the Republic or without, they are the source of strength that never fails. That this doctrine of Mélinism may make the price of food higher than it need be and that also it may hold back the advance of industry are trifling matters when compared with the stability of a nation that has so often been made to feel insecure. To those who stand amazed at the sight of the mounting surpluses of food caused by the C.A.P., at the piles of rotting fruit, at their sugar being sold in the world market at a price which is one-third of the cost of production, and at the French being ordered to feed back to their cows 6 per cent of the butter mountain, there is a short answer. It is that they do not understand France, neither her history, nor her temperament.

England—I say England deliberately—has never been afflicted by this fear of instability, yet if we become part of the EEC we will have to learn to live with Mélinism. Born of this most emotional creed are the most irrational parts of the C.A.P., and that is why any attempt by us to change it will be rebuffed

. .

by the French. Reform, when it comes, can be made only by a new philosophy.[1]

In seeking support for any change, we will turn in vain to the other members of the Community. Their belief in the existing policy may be founded upon other reasons which do not augur for any compromise. The Germans have had bequeathed to them by the *junkers* the quest for self-sufficiency, and this they know can be attained only by ultra-protectionism. Moreover, the two main parties, the Christian Democrats and Social Democrats, are pretty evenly balanced, which makes it worth their while to pay heed to the votes of several million farmers.

In the case of Italy, she has one-quarter of her working population employed in agriculture, compared with 40 per cent in 1950. This transplanting of millions has been fraught with political danger. It has given her Communist Party a position of considerable influence, and any further transfer of her population to the industrial areas will aggravate the danger to political stability. This danger will be naturally still worse if the work available in those areas does not provide a higher standard of living, and of that there is little certainty. Italy's present rate of industrial expansion cannot be accelerated to avert political risk; and therefore the 25 per cent of her population who remain on the land must be assured of a reasonable livelihood, although the price may be high.

The Netherlands has a well-organised and articulate farming community that is determined to hold its position. Drawn from them is Dr Sicco Mansholt himself, whose plans for reform, entitled "Agriculture 1980", are still as far from being carried out as when they were first published in 1968. Even his earlier proposals contained in the so-called Green Bible of 1960, which would have been only a modest piece of structural reform, were rejected by the member-countries. Despite the furore, all Dr Mansholt proposed was to get, as he put it, "the farmers in our six countries to do what the British and Americans did 50 years ago". Moreover, the Netherlands is one of the two countries, France being the other, which gets much more out of the Community's agricultural funds than she puts in, and so it is very much in her interests to maintain the *status quo*.

Belgium is so thrilled to have her own capital made the heart

[1] *Une France sans paysans* by Michel Gervais, Claude Servolin and Jean Weil; Edition du Seuil, Paris, 1965.

of what the eurocrats call "Europe" that she is forever silent on this and every other issue, lest dissension should cause her to lose this, her first *aggrandissement*. And Luxembourg is also silent, but for a reason that can never be her fault.

The forces in the Community that are opposed to agricultural reform, except on the periphery, are implacable. They have on their side the sturdy belligerence of which only a peasantry is capable, a lobby of enormous influence prompted by 12 per cent of the electorate, a century of Mélinism, and political reasons special to France, Germany, Italy, Holland, and Belgium—to them all except Luxembourg.

Changes in C.A.P. may be agreed upon, but to expect them to be carried out for a very long time is unrealistic and also dangerous to the political stability of the Community. Dr Mansholt has made 1980 the target date for his current plan; most students of the scene would say that even 1990 would border upon optimism.

Mr Anthony Barber had no alternative but to be wholly practical and give his assurance, at the outset of the negotiations, that the U.K. would accept the C.A.P. in its present form. Thus, it must be stated that, should we choose to enter the EEC, so far as its policy for agriculture goes, we have got to love it or lump it.

To love it will be perversion; to lump it, burdensome. We all know the awful dilemma of the shot-gun marriage : either the man marries the bride he will never love or he pays her a lot of money for nothing more in return. With the C.A.P. it is worse; to put it crudely, we marry the bride and we keep the brat—paying a lot of money and getting nothing in return. To assess how unlovable is the bride and how costly the brat is the purpose of this essay.

To describe in detail how the C.A.P. works would be tedious and unnecessary.[1] The arguments against it are founded upon the premises that to belong to the Community we must subscribe to some form of Common Agricultural Policy, that is to say, each member-country must have the same policy for its agriculture, and that, whatever form it takes, the aim will be self-sufficiency to be attained by a high level of protectionism.

---

[1] Of the several short publications on the subject, the most accurate and impartial is "The Agricultural Policy of the U.K. and EEC", published by U.K. Farming Representative, Barclays Bank, 52 Lombard Street, London, E.C.3.

If the rest of the world is short of food, the pursuit of self-sufficiency is positively praiseworthy. Those who formulated the C.A.P. were justified in believing that there was then a need to stimulate the growing of more food. However emotive statistics were being issued by the former administration of the Food and Agriculture Organisation—for example, that half the world was suffering from malnutrition—without adding that their yardstick was the eating habits of Londoners and Parisians. Little did those pedlars of gloom realise the harm that was to be done by their ludicrous exaggerations. According to the F.A.O. now, beef is the only major temperate food for which demand will put pressure upon supplies.

No one would have believed a decade ago, when they were working out the C.A.P., that the 1970s would witness the low-cost producers of food beginning to search for markets in the world. For us it is a serious matter, because 80 per cent of our trade is outside the EEC, and the greater part of our exports go across the seas to the countries where these low-cost producers are to be found. More serious still is the effect upon the growth of world trade. This growth, upon which the new wealth of the world depends, cannot be maintained unless more trade is liberated by pulling down, as gradually as is necessary, the barriers that now exist. Of all the barriers none will prove in the 1970s to be as intractable as the C.A.P.

The following table shows how self-sufficient the EEC is already compared with Britain.

Production of almost all these commodities is rising every year,

	EEC	BRITAIN
Wheat	115%	65%
Butter	110%	8%
Sugar	105%	33%
Vegetables	105%	80%
Milk	100%	100%
Pigmeat	100%	55%
Cheese	100%	45%
Poultry	100%	98%
Eggs	99%	98%
Fruit	90%	45%
Beaf and veal	90%	75%
Lamb and goat meat	85%	35%

so that even if the most rigorous of Dr Mansholt's proposals were carried out by the target date of 1980, there would still be considerable surpluses for several years to come. Of the three in which the Community are not self-sufficient, beef is the only one where there is an appreciable need for imports (very little veal is imported); lamb is not a significant market, and in the case of fruit, the 10 per cent deficiency is accounted for by bananas and citrus fruits because apples, pears, grapes and soft fruit are in surplus.

The Vedel Commission[1] has dismissed Dr Mansholt's plan as *derisoire*. It has had to admit, however, that the rapid improvements in farming methods will lead to far greater surpluses of food. It also recognises that there will be a still greater expansion of production if farms become fewer and larger as they are now tending to be.

These surpluses have already become a headache to the Community; but to primary producers elsewhere, who depend upon a narrow world market where prices are treacherous, they are both a headache and a heartache. More strictly, it is the Community's policy of turning these surpluses into subsidised exports that has caused this heartfelt anger and resentment in many countries, not least of all in the Commonwealth.

Let us see why it is so. Because the C.A.P. is an agricultural policy common to all the Six, prices must be common to all farmers within the Community, and although there are some regional variations to make up for the cost of distribution, the prices are fixed at the lowest common denominator of efficiency. Accordingly, producers of almost every kind of food are assured of a livelihood. If a farmer cannot find a market for what he produces, the Community intervenes to buy it from him at an intervention price; and while this is lower than the market price, it provides a fair return for all but the most inefficient.

Much of the surplus fruit—the pears and apples—can be left to rot, but the mountains of wheat, sugar, cheese and butter stubbornly refuse to evaporate into thin air. To store for future consumption would be futile; thus to export to other countries

---

[1] It consists of officials of the French Ministry of Agriculture and agricultural experts of distinction. Their report, "Prospective à long terme de l'agriculture Français 1968-1985" was published by the French Ministry in 1969.

has become imperative. To do so at world market prices without an enormous subsidy, has been shown by Dr Mansholt to be quite impossible. This he demonstrates by the following table[1] :

PRODUCER PRICE LEVEL FOR VARIOUS AGRICULTURAL PRODUCTS IN THE COMMUNITY COMPARED WITH PRICES ON WORLD MARKETS

Products	EEC price u.a./100 kg.	World market price u.a./100 kg.*	Percentage difference between EEC price and world price
	1	2	3
Wheat other than durum	10,73	5,79	185
Hard wheat	16,14	8,07	200
Husked rice	17,96	15,34	117
Barley	9,07	5,67	160
Maize	9,01	5,63	160
White sugar	22,35	5,10	438
Beef and veal	68,00	38,82	175
Pigmeat	56,71	38,56	147
Poultry	72,33	55,00	131
Eggs	51,14	38,75	132
Butter	187,44	47,25	397
Olive Oil	115,62	69,84	166
Oilseeds	20,19	10,11	200

1. Including direct subsidies to producers of durum wheat, olive oil and oilseeds.
2. Prices to wholesalers.
3. Not for all products.

* Until a common currency is agreed upon, expenditure is expressed in "units of account" and these have exactly the same value as the U.S. dollar.

If one sets aside the not very significant commodity of husked rice as well as eggs, poultry and pigmeat, where demand meets supply, one finds that the farmer in the EEC receives for his produce a price that is very considerably more than what it is in the world market, anything from 60 per cent more to a price 438 per cent more. Apart from making the consumer eat more expensively than is necessary, it causes the export of the

[1] Annex 12 of the Memorandum on the Reform of Agriculture in the EEC, i.e. "The Mansholt Plan". His figures are for the period 1967-68: the percentage differences are still much the same.

surpluses to be a most costly business. The sale of French butter in Hong Kong at two shillings a pound may not be typical, but there are plenty of other examples of a sensitive market being suddenly undermined by the EEC. The disposal of their million tons of surplus sugar has played havoc with the world price, and it was a major factor in causing it to fall at one point to £18 a ton. That is about half the cost of producing a ton of sugar in countries that can grow it the most efficiently!

It is not necessary to labour the point that for several developing countries sugar is the principal crop; unless they can find a place in the international sugar market at a reasonable price, millions of people will be needlessly impoverished.

The United States, Canada and Australia are low-cost producers of wheat, but they have been forced to restrict their production because the world market has been disrupted. The C.A.P., because it has encouraged a surplus of several million tons, must have a large part of the blame for this. Australia and New Zealand are the most efficient producers of milk, butter and cheese. In the world they have fairly similar shares of our market for butter and cheese. Australia's future has not been included in the negotiations, yet New Zealand's has. However, the latter's dairy farmers should not be too optimistic. M. Couve de Murville has put it very crisply :

If any peasant farmer was to be unemployed as a result of Britain's entry into the EEC it would be a New Zealand peasant farmer, not a French one.

We may persuade the Community to agree to some concession for the New Zealanders during the transitional period of entry, but a stay of execution will add little to their peace of mind. Unless some permanent agreement is reached to enable New Zealand to enter our market after the transitional period has ended, ruin will face many thousands of the most efficient farmers in the world.

For other countries, with whom we trade and need to trade, the effect will come later. Right across Asia and into Africa the green revolution is getting under way. New varieties of rice can increase yields three times over and recently discovered varieties of wheat can grow on soil regarded hitherto as quite unsuitable. China, for example, has become a major wheat producer and will

be growing enough to provide 23 kilograms per head of her population in 1975. Even India is likely to overcome the problem of
feeding her millions in little more than a decade hence. Despite
the huge growth in the size of the human race, before the end of
the 1980s there will be no shortage of cereals grown even in those
areas where starvation is today the common cause of death; and
throughout the rest of the world surpluses of this primary
foodstuff will be inevitable.

In 1975 there will be a total exportable surplus of wheat in the
world of no less than 21 million metric tons.[1] In the case of sugar
the world's trade exportable surplus will then be as much as
7 million metric tons.

Not only arable crops but livestock production also will be
transformed out of all recognition. It may have taken our own
farmers a long time to adopt some of these intensive and highly
productive methods, but for most of them the research has now
been done, the experiments completed, and the lessons learnt; it
does not take so long for them to be exported. Even in remote
villages in Central Africa the battery chicken-house has become
commonplace; and in most of the islands of the West Indies,
sophisticated systems of pig breeding have been working for
several years.

The developing countries, especially those in the Commonwealth, have a market for our goods which could be potentially
vast. This potential cannot be reached if they are unable to buy
our exports; and this is exactly what is happening. Two factors
are gradually worsening the terms of trade for them. The first is
the rate of inflation which is making our goods—indeed all manufactures from developed countries—even more expensive for them
to buy. The other is a steady decline in the price they receive for
the food and raw materials that they themselves put on the world
market. It is painfully obvious that if the cost of one's imports
goes up while the cost of one's own exports goes down, there can
be no hope of expanding trade. The United Nations Monthly
Bulletin of Statistics provides enough material to show that this is
so. Mr Colin Clark, the former Director of the Agricultural
Economics Research Institute, Oxford, has drawn upon these
figures[2] to show that over a ten-year period the price of manufac-

[1] Agricultural Commodities: Projections for 1975 and 1985: F.A.O.,
Rome, 1967.
[2] "Too Much Food?", *Lloyds Bank Review*, January 1970.

tures purchased by the developing countries has risen 14 per cent, while the price of food and raw materials sold by them has fallen 10 per cent. I have not found it possible to make any accurate assessment of the extent that this fall in prices is due to the C.A.P. However, it can be said with absolute certainty that the problem will get worse, and as it gets worse so will the growth in world trade be curtailed.[1]

The money spent to subsidise the export of the Community's surpluses comes from F.E.O.G.A.[2] In the future this is likely to account for no less than 95 per cent of its new federal-type budget. It is administered from Brussels and its ramifications have become so complex that it accounts for a large number of the 7,000 officials now employed by the EEC. Another notable fact is that of the many thousands of regulations that have cascaded out of Brussels—all of which have the force of law— more than three-quarters of them relate to F.E.O.G.A.

By the time we can be a full member, F.E.O.G.A. will obtain all its income from the Community's now federal-type budget. All members of the Community will hand over the whole of their revenue derived from import levies on food, the whole of the revenue from the common external tariff and the yield of up to 1 per cent of a value added tax, which all members must adopt.

Not all the revenue is disbursed in buying up food surpluses or in subsidising their export abroad. The "O" in F.E.O.G.A. stands for "Orientation" or what we would call guidance; and this part is similar to our system of farm improvement grants. It has ten main schemes upon which it is now spending money. They are the modernising of backward farms, the rationalisation of the dairy industry, the marketing of fruit and vegetables, research into the improvement of meat, new irrigation, the productivity of the labour force, drainage schemes, the development of wine growing, converting marginal farms into forestry and the production of olive oil. It is intended to limit expenditure from the guidance section to about $250 million a year. This

---

[1] The problem has indeed got worse since this was written. I am indebted to the Statistical Section of the Research Division of the House of Commons library for working out the latest figures for a ten-year period. The average price of food and raw materials exported by developing countries has fallen now by 11 per cent while the price of manufactures that they have imported has risen by 16 per cent.

[2] *Fonds Européan d'Orientation et de Garantie Agricole*, the European Agricultural Guidance and Guarantee Fund.

makes it only a small part of the total fund, about 3 per cent, but even this amount, by improving the methods of production, will tend to aggravate the problem of the surpluses, and thus add to the burden to be carried by the guarantee section.

When exports are subsidised by the guarantee section there are two obvious consequences that have to follow. The first is that they create very unfair competition for the efficient and low-cost producers of the world who are often in countries that are largely or wholly dependent upon agriculture as the mainstay of their own exports. They also are a burden to the Community which is much greater than most people recognise. Dr Mansholt has shown[1] that before the C.A.P. was introduced the total expenditure on market support for agriculture by all the Six was $495 million, but five years of C.A.P. caused an increase of more than 300 per cent, to $1,519 million. For 1970 it is likely to have doubled again, and all the evidence points to an annual increase of about $500 million for several years to come. This is very far from being the total cost of supporting the farmers of the Six.

The United States Department of Agriculture[2] has estimated that the extra cost to the consumer in the EEC caused by his having to buy his food at an artificially high price came to about $6,400 million, the difference between the price he pays and world prices. This is in addition to the cost of farm support and agricultural expenditure by the governments of the Six. The three items together make the total cost of the C.A.P. some $14,000 million. This latter figure has been calculated by Dr Oscar Zaglits, formerly Counsellor for Agricultural Affairs of the U.S. Mission to the EEC. $80 per head of the population may not seem much, but as the burden is effectively on the backs of those who are employed outside agriculture, the true economic cost is considerably more.

Dr Nicholas Kaldor[3] has also added up a bill which is well-nigh astronomical; to the cost of market support he has added the difference between the Community price for food and the world price and all the indirect payments and other subsidies

[1] Annex 21 of the Memorandum on the Reform of Agriculture in the EEC.

[2] "The Costs of the Common Agricultural Policy to the European Community Consumers", Washington, 1969.

[3] In a paper read to the Internation Press Institute in Paris on January 13th, 1970, and reported in full in the *New Statesman,* April 3rd, 1970.

to their farmers. His result is $15,000 million. It is 4 per cent of
the GNP of the EEC. As he points out, it is two-thirds of their
expenditure on defence and one-tenth of all forms of public
expenditure, including transfer payments. According to my calculations, if we were to spend, directly and indirectly, the same
proportion of our GNP on the support of agriculture, the cost
would come to £1,600,000,000. Alternatively, one-tenth of our
public expenditure comes to £2,000,000,000. In other words,
they spend proportionately twice as much on supporting farmers
as we spend upon housing; again proportionately, they give to
their farmers over and above what they need pay for their food
nearly as much as what we spend upon public education. Once
more proportionately in terms of GNP the price they pay for
Mélinism is just about the same as the total amount that we pay
for all forms of our national defence. Before we dismiss it as folly,
let us recall the philosophy that is behind it: Mélinism, for both
France and Italy, is probably their most important arm of
defence, internally, if not externally. It is a high but necessary
price to pay for political stability.

Paying more for our food is very far from being the only cost
of the C.A.P. Opponents of entry into the EEC have their supply
of adrenalin consumed by the constant repetition of the charge
that they base their whole case upon this one point.

The White Paper estimated a rise of 18 per cent to 26 per cent
in food prices—about £1 a week for the ordinary family whose
income is the national industrial average—and this must have its
effect upon wage claims and make it necessary to increase all
social security payments. All that is obvious and needs no
emphasis here. The claim that the increase in the standard of
living will make good the increase in the cost of living is amply
rebutted elsewhere in this symposium.

There are, however, four other costs which we will have to
face:

1. The cost to the Exchequer of payments into F.E.O.G.A.
2. The cost in terms of foreign exchange.
3. The cost in loss of trade with our existing suppliers of food.
4. The cost to our own farmers.

The first three overlap, but each is a cost to a separate part of
the economy, and for that reason they deserve to be looked at
differently. As to the first of them, most of the original estimates

as to what it would cost us have gone not a little awry. Lord Walston[1] assessed that our Exchequer payment would be some £250 million. In arriving at this he assumed that by 1973 the total cost of the C.A.P. would be no more than £1,750 million, that the Mansholt Plan would be put into effect and that various other steps would be taken to reduce the production of surpluses.

On the basis that the Community's budget will need revenue of $4,500 million (£1,875 million) in 1977, taxation within this country will be £468 million. This is the official estimate but its accuracy depends, of course, upon whether its expenditure can be contained in the estimated figure. If it exceeds that figure, increases will be necessary in the common external tariff (which will be contrary to the General Agreement on Tariffs and Trade) or in the import levies (which will put up the price of food) or in the rate of the value added tax. Whatever the revenue required proves to be, it will be income lost to the Exchequer which could otherwise be used to lower the burden of taxation upon the British public. £468 million is the equivalent of about 4p on the rate of income tax.

The cost in terms of foreign exchange is not necessarily the same amount. This will be the net outflow; it is a cost borne not by the individual taxpayer, but by the country as a whole in our balance-of-payments. It is the cost that stunts our economic growth.

In the ordinary way a loss on our balance-of-payments is not a loss of wealth, because food, raw materials or manufactured goods have come into the country in exchange for it. The cost under this heading, however, is quite different: whether the amount proves to be large or small, it will be unrequited, in that we recieve no benefit in return. The White Paper of 1967[2] suggested that "the net cost to the U.K. balance-of-payments of applying the EEC's agricultural arrangements as they stand might be in the range of £175 million to £250 million annually". Since then these "agricultural arrangements" have become a good deal more costly and our own devaluation has lowered the value of that number of £s. It is therefore an assumption that the net cost of the C.A.P. will be not less than the same as our

[1] "Farmgate to Brussels", Fabian Research Series. A pamphlet sympathetic to the Common Agricultural Policy. Unfortunately many of its facts are now out of date.

[2] Common Agricultural Policy of the EEC. Commd. 3274.

contribution to the Community's budget. Some commentators have put it considerably higher; as Mr Samuel Brittain, Economics Editor of the *Financial Times*, says, "the range now appears in the £500-£1,000 million bracket".

It is to the third of these four costs that the least attention has been paid, and yet it may prove to have the gravest effects. It should be self-evident that if we cut our imports from the United States, Canada, South Africa, Australia, New Zealand and the West Indies they will be driven to accepting fewer of our exports. That we are to buy less from them and more from the EEC once we are a member cannot be denied; the understanding in fact is a condition of our entry into the Community, certainly as seen by the French. The Paris correspondent of *The Times* has summed it up : "The French will support our entry if they believe that we have adopted the underlying principle of the Common Market, that of Community preference." Referring to Britain he goes on : "This is the touchstone of her final unrestricted conversion to Europe, both in the economic and political sense. It will determine Britain's attitude on sterling as much as the reorientation of her trade patterns. This is what Community preference is all about, over and above its immediate agricultural significance."[1]

In bald terms, the French farmer must have preference over the Australian, the Italian over the Canadian, the German over those in New Zealand. Defensive steps have already been taken; the sad fact that Australia and Canada have had to cut back the production of their cheaper wheat has been noted above. The New Zealand Government has had to force her exporters to divert their supplies of lamb from Britain to other markets. This is done by allocating to each exporter a quota for our market and if the quota is exceeded a penalty is imposed upon him. That our friends in New Zealand should actually be punished for sending us the cheap meat that our housewives would like to buy— causing them to buy more expensive meat from elsewhere—is nothing short of craziness, for which we ourselves are wholly to blame.

The other side of the coin is that our exporters to these countries are finding that orders that they might have had are going to Japan, the United States and elsewhere. A Pacific Free Trade Area (PAFTA) is no longer a remote possibility, and once it comes about our exporters will be the ones to lose the most.

[1] *The Times*, December 22nd, 1970.

So far, the cost to us may be only a bagatelle, yet once any transitional period has expired and we have become full members of the EEC its magnitude should daunt even the most ecstatic of the marketeers. The Commonwealth Producers Organisation has provided some figures which have not been challenged.[1] According to them, the ending of the preference system would cause the British export trade to lose a minimum of £200 million a year in Canada, Australia and New Zealand alone. To this should be added the loss of invisible earnings in shipping and insurance of between £50 million and £100 million. This is, of course, but a small fraction of the total trade as the total value of our exports to the Commonwealth Preference area come to £2,200 million and in return we receive about a quarter of our food from them. Obviously not all our food, not even the temperate foods, will come instead from the farmers of the Six if we enter the EEC; but just a mere 5 per cent switch of imports from the Commonwealth to the Six will mean a transfer of many £ millions of trade. For every £ spent on buying our food from the EEC instead of our present suppliers, there is likely to be a £ lost to our present export trade. Is there any possibility that this cost be less than £100 million? Or will it be very much more?

The final cost is the one borne by our own farmers. If the proposed reforms are put into operation everyone in agriculture, on both sides of the channel, will feel the chilly winds. Dr Mansholt has stated[2] that consumption will guide and limit production via the price mechanism, with the result that agricultural markets can work in a more "normal" way! When he goes on to explain that this will avoid the structural surpluses, he makes it as plain as the proverbial pikestaff that his reforms will make farm prices go plummeting down.

Whatever may be said or even agreed upon, it remains politically undesirable, if not dangerous, for those reforms to be carried out. In theory our own farmers, being on the whole much more efficient than those on the Continent, should be the beneficiaries of the system. The practice does not match the theory because our farmers have long ceased to be homogeneous. Modern methods of husbandry, by causing the demise of mixed farming,

[1] "Britain and the EEC", a pamphlet published by them at 25 Victoria Street, London, S.W.1.
[2] Page 30, Memorandum on the Reform of Agriculture in the European Economic Community.

have made it impossible to make general statements about the interests of farmers as a whole. Broadly speaking, those in agriculture now specialise either in livestock or in arable crops. A third category, those in horticulture, represent 10 per cent of the industry and they are particularly vulnerable on account of the climate. The former two have a fundamental conflict of interest. The livestock man, whether in dairying, pigs, or poultry, gives his stock sophisticated compound feeding-stuffs. These are by far the biggest item of his expenditure, perhaps 70 per cent or 80 per cent of his on-costs. Between 75 per cent and 85 per cent of the compound will consist of various cereals. While the farmer specialising in arable crops will gain when cereal prices rise, the specialist in livestock manifestly stands to lose a great deal. For various reasons neither the target nor intervention prices in the EEC compensate for the higher price of compounds. Those in dairying will have to face the surpluses of butter and cheese. Our Milk Marketing Board has said[1] that our producers might receive about 1p a gallon more if the EEC target price were attained, but it adds that milk would become relatively less profitable than at present compared with beef and cereals. In this category, although working under different conditions, are the hill farmers. Their profit is usually equal to the subsidies they receive, and these have a doubtful future in the Community.

Most arable farmers in East Anglia are heavily dependent upon potatoes, wheat and sugar beet. While the two latter will have to compete with steadily mounting surpluses, the potatoes will compete with those grown in more favourable climates, although the yellower-fleshed varieties of the Continent may not be so popular with us. There is one group that may be no worse off, the barley-and-beef men. Unfortunately, many of them have been growing their barley continuously on the same land for many years without a break. It was thought that modern methods would enable this practice to go on indefinitely, but the need for more frequent break-crops has become most apparent.[2] Nor can one be optimistic about beef. The cheapest and easiest way to expand production is by fattening calves from a larger

---

[1] "Prospects for Milk in the EEC", May 1970.

[2] "Modern Farming and the Soil", published by H.M. Stationery Office and compiled by a panel of farmers and scientists chosen by the Minister of Agriculture. It provides irrefutable evidence that barley-growers must reconsider this crop.

dairy herd, but this will only add to the surplus of milk. The alternative is more Herefords and others of the beef breeds, which will make for more expensive meat—too dear for the vast majority.

Our own farmers receive more than £100 million a year in various improvement grants. They are the equivalent of the grants from the guidance section of F.E.O.G.A. and it is significant that the total sum spent on "guidance" is the same in the United Kingdom as in the EEC. The difference is in the number of beneficiaries. In Britain about 200,000 farmers are eligible to receive a part of this £100 million; in the EEC nearly the same amount has to be shared among nearly twelve times the number of farmers. One could be pretty sure that very little of the guidance section of F.E.O.G.A. would come to the United Kingdom, while, of course, the existing system of improvement grants would come to an end. The net cost of entry for our farmers is therefore unlikely to be less than £100 million, but it could be much more.

It is certain that the "European" lobby will try to make the cost of entry one of the focal-points of debate. Whether one can quantify the price at a total of £100 million or more than £1,000 million will provide ample scope for a long and circular debate; out of it will emerge their argument, what does it matter if the entry is our destiny; if the price is high, can it not be paid over many years of membership in a dynamic market?

The answer comes from Brussels itself. They have a saying there which is often repeated. It is that entering the Community is like getting on to a moving train. The simile is particularly apt for the British people. Before we board a train, there are two questions that we ask ourselves. One is, can we afford the fare? But the other is much more important : will it take us where we want to go? If Mr Rippon will forgive me putting it in personal terms, when he goes to Kings Cross to catch his train to Hexham, he does not want to be bundled by an officious porter into the non-stop express to Aberdeen. For him to be told that he can afford the fare is not the slightest consolation, because he does not want to go all the way up to the North of Scotland, whatever the price of the journey may be.

It is the dilemma that now faces the British people, who are on the point of being swept into the express to Federal Europe (the train may stop on the way, but the passengers cannot get out).

The cost of the fare is important, but it is whether we want that particular destination that really counts.

So far as agriculture is concerned, the aim of the train journey is in sight : self-sufficiency and a switch in trade, which for us means more trade with the Six and less across the seas with the Commonwealth and our other markets.

It is a destination that can only be reached by a very high level of protectionism. A degree of protection may be necessary to safeguard a vulnerable industry such as agriculture. However the inordinate degree demanded by the C.A.P. must have the effect of cutting back the growth of world trade. Of that there can be no doubt. This is where the long-term danger lies for a country, like ours, that depends so much upon world trade. Eighty per cent of our trade is across the seas : how much of it are we willing to lose to get across the Channel?

The train that we should be catching is the one that takes us along the journey of open trade to the destination of an open world. Mr Rippon should realise that we cannot combine a policy of liberalising world trade with membership of the Community, no more than he can catch both his train to Hexham and the non-stop to Aberdeen.

AN INDUSTRIALIST'S VIEWPOINT

by Sir John Hunter
Chairman, Swan-Hunter (Shipbuilders)

I T I S N O T my purpose in this essay to discuss the political case
for and against entry. I need only say that British industry within
the EEC would be subjected, both in the economic policies with
which it had to live, and in some cases in the detailed regulations
to which it would have to submit, either to a bureaucracy in
Brussels or to a federal parliament. Industrialists, like every voter
in Britain, have to ask themselves whether they want either of
these things, since they must have one or the other if Britain joins
the EEC.

Advocates of British entry claim that it would be beneficial to
the economy in general and to industry in particular. As I see it
the contrary is the case : British entry, on any terms in the least
likely to be accepted by the Six, would make Britain's economic
position significantly worse than it is now.

Let us leave aside for the moment the rise in British costs due
to rising food prices occasioned by our acceptance of the Common Agricultural Policy. Since the EEC's common external tariff
is on average lower than Britain's tariffs, the result of their
abolition must be that the EEC would gain rather more than us
on the deal. We would also be more vulnerable to competition
from the rest of the world in our home market once we had
substituted the EEC's common external tariff for our own. There
are of course British industries which, despite this weighting of
advantage against Britain, are confident that they would gain
more in new export sales than they would lose to EEC competitors in their home market. This confidence is justified primarily
in the case of companies whose major potential export market
would be the Six, since companies looking to the EFTA and
Commonwealth markets as well are going to find their prospects

diminished rather than enhanced by EEC entry, as they lose
preferential tariff treatment. Against the optimistic industries
must be set those whose chances of selling more to the EEC are
dwarfed by their prospects of seeing their share of the home
market eroded by imports from the EEC.

This is not necessarily an argument against industrial free
trade among the developed nations. Indeed, it can be argued,
against those who see the removal of EEC tariffs on British
exports as the main advantage of entry, that those tariffs are
likely to come down gradually in any case, along with those of
other industrialised nations, as a result of further multilateral
negotiations under GATT auspices. But it is one thing to envisage a gradual reduction of tariffs, and welcome it, and quite
another to embrace their complete removal in five years in the
case of exports from some of one's strongest competitors. Nor
should one accept the marketeers' argument that EEC entry will
force British industry to be more competitive. Customs unions
comprising relatively stronger and weaker partners inevitably
favour the former, as the relative fortunes of the north and south
in Italy after unification show very clearly; and many British
industries might well be forced out rather than forced on.

It does not need a very long look at the late 1950s and 1960s
to appreciate that British industry has not been investing enough
on new equipment and techniques, and that the prime reason for
this has been uncertainty about future demand—uncertainty
engendered by the familiar stop-go sequence in demand management. That sequence has been a response to balance-of-payments
considerations. It is plain common sense for industrialists to raise
their voices against a policy which will intensify it; and Britain's
entry into the EEC must intensify it.

In the first place a considerable sum will have to be paid across
the exchanges to the EEC authorities, essentially to prop up the
living standards of inefficient French and German peasants; a
sum which will become much larger once the transitional period
is over. Without at this stage forecasting exact amounts, it is clear
that Britain will be obliged to hand over several hundred million
pounds a year on this score alone.

The marketeers' preferred response when this point is emphasised is to say that an increase in Britain's growth rate by one
percentage point would suffice to pay "the price of entry". It is
not easy to understand how people with some claims to economic

literacy can put forward this argument. For they are not only
begging the question of whether British entry into the EEC
would permit a higher growth rate—which is after all the central
question of the whole argument—but are also assuming that a
higher growth rate would mean a corresponding improvement in
the balance-of-payments sufficient to permit our subsidy of continental peasants. In fact an improvement in Britain's GNP
growth rate has tended in the past to be followed fairly swiftly by
a worsening balance-of-payments situation.

It is indeed astonishing to hear the advocates of British entry
talking about higher growth when one recalls at what cost in real
growth the previous government made possible the heavy current
account surpluses of 1969 and 1970. For what we are being
asked to do is to accept, on top of our still heavy debt-repayment
obligations, a further continuing and heavy call upon our
foreign exchange reserves. In other words, we shall have to go on
earning a massive current account surplus. This surplus can only
be accumulated, as in the past, at the expense of growth.

This involves a real danger that, so far from being stimulated
by uncurbed competition with the Six, British industry will be
badly hit. For if the economic conditions of the last three years
are going to be extended on into the 1970s industry is not going to
invest in the way that is necessary to meet European competition.
And it would be wrong to assume that because productivity will
therefore rise slowly and because demand will be choked back so
as to generate the surplus, wage claims are going to be moderate
accordingly. All the current evidence points to the contrary. It
follows that Britain's competitiveness can only be maintained by
heavy investment in greater productivity so that wage claims can
be absorbed. That is only likely to come in an economy relatively
free from balance-of-payments constraints, not in one that is
wilfully taking on heavy new foreign exchange burdens.

The argument so far has concerned only British trade with the
Six; this accounts for only one-fifth of total British exports. What
about the remainder of our trade? Firstly, entry constitutes a
threat to British sales in the vital U.S. market. The fact that the
U.S. Senate killed a protectionist trade bill at the end of 1970 by
no means implies that the danger of protectionism there is at an
end. Indeed it is probable that a similar bill will be introduced in
the course of 1971; and, although the inspiration of the rejected
bill was concern about Japanese textile exports to the U.S., there

is no doubt that U.S. protectionists are making use of, and will continue to make use of, resentment in America about EEC policies. This resentment centres round the EEC's Common Agricultural Policy, which limits U.S. exports of farm produce, and the EEC policy of concluding preferential trade agreements with third countries, which discriminate against U.S. exports in general. Both grievances would be made more intense if Britain were to join the EEC, in the first case simply by an extension of the Common Agricultural Policy's field of operations, in the second because British entry would be accompanied by the conclusion of preferential agreements between the EEC and a number of African Commonwealth countries. The danger is that the EEC's behaviour, and Britain's complicity in it, would help to turn the U.S. away from the liberal trade policies it pursued in the 1960s. This could only result in a shrinkage in the total market available to British industrialists.

Accession to the EEC would also mean a loss of export markets in the Commonwealth and South Africa, since Britain's withdrawal of Commonwealth preference, a necessary condition of entry, would be quickly followed by a similar withdrawal of the preferences now enjoyed by British exporters in these markets. The marketeers tend to shrug this off as unimportant, yet the C.B.I. pro-market report admits that the loss of trade to Britain in this respect alone would balance any gains that could be expected in the EEC market.

The marketeers' apparent contempt for Commonwealth trade relies heavily on the projection of past trends into the future, both in the sense that they expect EEC growth to continue at the same high rate as in the 1950s, and to a lesser extent in the 1960s, and in the sense that they expect Britain to hold a declining share of a less rapidly expanding Commonwealth market. They could well be wrong on both counts. There is little statistical evidence to suggest that G.N.P. growth rates in the six EEC countries have been higher on average than they would have been had the Treaty of Rome not been signed. The more we are persuaded that our future lies with six countries in a part of Western Europe, the less attention we shall pay to the developing countries of the Commonwealth, and in that case we shall tend to surrender our market share to competitors, including EEC competitors, who are not inhibited by an exclusive fixation on Western Europe. The virtues of careful attention to difficult markets is amply illustrated by the growth of British exports to Latin America by 60 per cent in three years. While the 1967 devaluation obviously helped here, the decisive factor was a refusal to acquiesce any longer in a fatalistic abandonment of the field to the West Germans and the Japanese. We can do it, but we shall not do it if we are hypnotised into concentrating on one-fifth of our export market and forgetting the remainder.

The other preferences British manufacturers would lose on entry are provided by EFTA. It is an organisation brushed aside by the marketeers, presumably because it lacks the federalist drive and overblown sense of destiny of the EEC; but it offers British industry free access to markets which boast some of the richest and most sophisticated consumers in the world. If Britain joined the EEC, it would lose that preference—in the case of Norway and Denmark, which would join if we did, because EEC countries would gain the preference against third countries which we now enjoy; in the case of Sweden and the other non-applicant EFTA countries, because we should again face, with our own costs increased, the tariffs the exporters of the Six face now while we enjoy free entry. This would represent a further shrinkage in the total market for British exports compared with what it would be if Britain did not join the EEC.

The argument so far has shown that the market for British industry would be smaller if Britain were part of the EEC than if it remained outside, despite any likely extra growth in sales to the Six. It suggests that at best only those firms whose prospects are very heavily weighted towards the markets of the Six—a minority—would benefit from entry. But even these firms, and those concerned primarily to defend home markets, cannot ignore the fact that British entry is in one important sense going to make all British industry less competitive at home, in EEC markets and in third markets. As I said at the beginning, Britain's acceptance of the EEC's Common Agricultural Policy is going to mean, according to official estimates, an increase in food prices of between 18 and 26 per cent. No doubt an attempt will be made to assure the public that the increase will be smaller than this; and indeed it will be, since the Government has already decided on a partial switch to the EEC system whereby farmers are subsidised by the consumer through import levies instead of by the general tax-payer through deficiency payments; thus part of the cost of EEC entry to the consumer will be paid in advance. Mr James Prior,

the Minister of Agriculture, has tried to gloss over the meaning of
this switch by talking of the present arrangements as a system of
food subsidies, whose abolition would be part of a process of
"standing on one's own two feet". In fact, the British consumer is
paying world market prices for his food, while British farmers are
being subsidised to make up for the extent to which they are
unable to produce at world prices. What is proposed for the
future is that the British consumer should pay an artificially high
price for his food.

There might indeed be some advantage to the industrialist in
the switch of policy while it is a purely British affair, since the
saving to the Treasury on deficiency payments and the revenue
accruing from food taxes might permit a reduction in corporate
taxation. Even this consolation will be notably diminished, however, when the full yield of the food import levies plus all our
customs revenues and part of the yield of VAT has to be handed
over to Brussels as it would have to be. And the major disadvantage remains. Given the period over which the increase in food
prices would be spread, the change, it is contended, would only
mean an additional increase in the cost of living of under 1 per
cent a year. But no country with Britain's inflationary and
balance-of-payments problems should willingly accept even that.
For the percentage increase mentioned above is an average for all
consumers : the bigger the proportion of its expenditure devoted
to food, the more a family's cost of living will be increased. The
lowest paid workers will be the hardest hit. The level of wage
claims of the lowest paid will be increased, and with it the level of
all settlements. Unless this inflated level of settlements takes place
within the context of an incomes policy which deliberately aims
to improve the relative position of the worst paid *vis-à-vis* the
better paid, which seems most unlikely, the upward pressure on
settlements is going to become general throughout industry as the
better paid seek to maintain differentials. Industrialists must
reconcile themselves, therefore, to the knowledge that entry into
the EEC is going to raise their costs considerably. It is impossible
to do more than guess what this means in terms of loss of
markets, but it will certainly make them more vulnerable to EEC
competition in the home market, making it even less likely that
Britain would make any net gain purely on trade with the EEC
countries; and it must mean substantial loss of markets to
competitors in third markets. The argument is strengthened by

the severe current squeeze on company profits, which leaves very little further room for absorbing higher costs.

This, then, is the "entrance fee" which the Government is apparently willing to pay in order to secure extremely nebulous long-term benefits, allegedly economic and political. There is no doubt that the sales of British industry outside this country would be lower after entry than they would be if we remained outside, and that sales to the home market would also be cut into by increased European competition. While this would probably not mean an absolute fall in the general level of industrial production, it would mean a lower rate of economic growth than we could have achieved otherwise. This effect would be reinforced by the sort of restrictive policies which would have to be imposed in order to generate a large current account for handing over to Brussels. The reward for this sacrifice, we are told, is higher growth in the long-term, as a result of the dynamic effect of increased competition and a "home market" of 300 million people. This argument needs close examination; for supposing Britain's growth rate were consistently lower in the first ten years of EEC membership than would have been the case were we not members, and then in the next ten years consistently higher, it would need to be a really high growth rate in that second ten years to bring us up to the point after twenty that we should have reached on our own—quite possibly a higher rate than the Six would then be achieving themselves. Thus even if membership did eventually generate this high rate of growth, after perhaps a decade of the frustrations and social tensions associated with low growth, it would only begin to pay real benefits after perhaps twenty years. Is this really the panacea for our ills?

The argument from "economies of scale", so often advanced as a reason for British entry, really only applies to a few industries such as aircraft production, and it is perfectly possible in these cases to come to ad-hoc arrangements, such as that for the Concorde. For the rest of industry, a "home market" of 300 million is not necessary for optimum efficiency, and in any case the EEC is still far from being a home market to its industrialists in that sense, and perhaps never will be, given the persistence of differing national characteristics. Bigness, in any case, is not all, as some industrialists caught up in the cult of mergers now realise. And where trans-national mergers are dictated by sound business reasons, there is precious little evidence to date that membership of the EEC facilitates them. What have the marketeers to come up with to compare with the Dunlop-Pirelli merger? This is no sort of evidence to advance the case for British entry. Indeed the only sort of merger now taking place within the EEC consists of U.S. companies buying up European companies. This is likely to work to Britain's disadvantage if we enter, as U.S. firms now basing themselves in Britain are likely, on British entry, to decide because of transport costs, on a location somewhere in the Ruhr-Belgium-N.E. France complex.

Opponents of British entry to the EEC are often asked what alternative to membership they propose. There are of course several well-known alternatives capable of achievement with patience and good-will. Since, however, the case is very strong for supposing that entry would limit our trade and stunt our growth, may one end by suggesting that the proper alternative to the adoption of a harmful course of action is not to adopt it.

PART TWO

The Domestic Implications

I V

THE DYNAMIC EFFECTS OF THE COMMON MARKET

by *Nicholas Kaldor*

Professor of Economics, Cambridge University: former Economic Adviser to the British Government.

I T I S G E N E R A L L Y agreed that the initial effects of joining the Common Market are likely to be unfavourable to Britain, mainly owing to the heavy cost of assuming the obligations of the Common Agricultural Policy. It is argued however that these unfavourable impact effects are likely to be more than offset by the long-term advantages—the so-called "dynamic effects" of membership. Last year's White Paper on *Britain and the European Communities*[1] described the nature of these advantages in the following terms :

> For industry and trade, the main consequences of United Kingdom membership of an enlarged community would be that we should form part of a Customs Union of up to 300 million people stretching from Scotland to Sicily and from the Irish Republic to the borders of Eastern Europe. Within this vast area, industrial products would move freely—without tariff or quota restrictions—as soon as any transitional period had been completed. And over the years ahead it would be the intention to convert this Customs Union into a full economic union by the progressive alignment and harmonisation of commercial policy, i.e., trading relations with third countries; of economic and fiscal policy; of company and patent law; of standards for industrial products . . . etc.
>
> The creation of such an enlarged and integrated European market would provide in effect a much larger and a much

[1] Cmnd. 4289, February 1970.

faster growing "home market" for British industry. It would provide the stimuli of much greater opportunities—and competition—than exist at present or would otherwise exist in future. There would be substantial advantage for British industry from membership of this new Common Market, stemming primarily from the opportunities for greater economies of scale, increased specialisation, a sharper competitive climate and faster growth. These may be described as the "dynamic effects" of membership on British industry and trade. It has not been found possible to measure the likely response of British industry to these new opportunities nor, therefore, the effects on our economic growth and balance of payments.[1]

In the concluding section the White Paper strikes an even more confident note about the "dynamic effects" resulting from membership of a "much larger and faster growing market":

This would open up to our industrial producers substantial opportunities for increasing export sales, while at the same time exposing them more fully to the competition of European industries. No way has been found of quantifying these dynamic effects but, if British industry responded vigorously to these stimuli, they would be considerable and highly advantageous. *The acceleration in the rate of growth of industrial exports could then outpace any increase in the rate of growth of imports* with corresponding benefits to the balance of payments. Moreover, *with such a response*, the growth of industrial productivity would be accelerated as a result of increased competition and the advantages derived from specialisation and larger scale production. This faster rate of growth of productivity would, in turn, accelerate the rate of growth of national production and real income.[2]

The same argument has been repeated in other documents[3] but without adding anything of substance to the case as presented in these quotations. There are frequent references to the fact that the countries of the EEC have experienced much higher growth

[1] Cmnd. 4289, paras 52-53.

[2] Cmnd. 4289, para 77. Italics not in the original.

[3] See for example, *Britain in Europe—A second industrial appraisal*, Confederation of British Industry, January 1970.

rates than Britain since the war, with the implication that if Britain formed part of the Community, her own growth rate would be assimilated to that of the other members. Since the rate of Britain's economic growth has been so much lower than that of the countries of the Common Market—around 3 per cent a year, in the period 1958-69, as against 5.4 per cent for the Six—this in itself would establish a strong presumption in favour of joining the Community.

But whether any such tendency can be presumed to exist or not is a matter that requires closer analysis of the causes of high and low growth rates, and of the effects of increased competition on growth. It cannot be taken for granted as a self-evident matter that the intensification of competition between different industrial regions brought about by a Customs Union will automatically enhance the rate of growth of *each* of the participating regions taken separately.[1]

Indeed, as the italicised passage of the White Paper indicates, the favourable effects on our growth rate depend on the hypothesis that opportunities created by the Common Market will lead to an acceleration in the rate of growth of industrial exports which will "outpace any increase in the rate of growth of imports". But what if the response were the other way round, with an acceleration in the rate of growth of imports that "outpaced" any increase in our exports? Or, if exports, instead of rising, fell in consequence? It could not then be maintained that the rate of growth of national production and real income would be higher as a result; on the contrary, the effect would be to make our rate of economic growth lower than it would be otherwise, or even to make it negative. The question, in other words, is not only one of

[1] There is certainly no evidence to show that the creation of the Common Market enhanced the rate of economic growth of *each* of the participating countries taken separately, or even of the area as a whole. The rate of economic growth of the Six countries taken together was lower in 1958-69 than in 1950-58; while the rates of growth of other OECD countries (both inside and outside Europe) were higher in the latter period than in the former. The formation of the Customs Union seems to have clearly benefited Italy (which increased its share of total trade in manufactured goods, both inside and outside the Community) and probably also Belgium, but there is no clear evidence in the case of the others. Cf. R. L. Major and associates, *Another Look at the Common Market,* National Institute Economic Review, November 1970, pp. 29-43. For reasons adduced below, the experience of the six countries is not necessarily relevant from the point of view of the effects of entry on Britain.

"quantifying" the magnitude of these "dynamic effects" but of discovering, in the first place, whether they should be entered on the credit side or the debit side.

The White Paper is certainly correct in suggesting that the "dynamic effects" on our growth rate are likely to be far more important over a run of years than the "impact effects", however large the latter may be. An increase in our growth rate by 1 per cent—that is, from say 3 to 4 per cent a year—is likely to compensate for the initial cost of entry in three years even if the latter is as much as 3 per cent of our national income, or £1,200 million a year. Conversely, a 1 per cent diminution in our growth rate is likely to double the annual cost of membership in three years, treble it in six years, and so on.

The basic question therefore is whether entry into the EEC is likely to have a favourable effect on our growth rate or an adverse one. This question cannot be answered without considering the more fundamental question of what makes the rate of growth of productivity relatively fast in some countries and relatively slow in others.

The argument that follows is wholly in accord with the White Paper's own intellectual approach to the problem—the question is only whether the White Paper's optimistic conclusions concerning our growth rate follow from their premises.

Causes of High and Low Growth Rates

There is a substantial amount of evidence in favour of the view that causes of high and low rates of productivity growth of various countries or regions are closely bound up with the rates of growth of manufacturing production. There are two main reasons for this. The first is that economies of large-scale production, due to ever-increasing differentiation and subdivision of processes, are peculiar to manufacturing ("processing activities") as distinct from either primary production (agriculture or mining) or tertiary production (transport, distribution and miscellaneous services). The second is that in the sectors other than manufacturing (chiefly in agriculture but also in services) there is in most countries a considerable surplus of labour (some kind of "disguised unemployment") so that when the manufacturing sector expands and draws more labour from other sectors, these other sectors are not forced to curtail their output : on the contrary their output will tend to increase if they provide goods or services that are complementary (or ancillary) to manufacturing activities. Hence the faster manufacturing output expands, the faster productivity will rise, both in the manufacturing sector and in the non-manufacturing sectors.[1]

Added to these is the fact that in "capitalist" economies at any rate the increase in industrial capital necessary for an expansion of output is largely self-generated : the more production expands, the greater is the inducement to invest in the expansion of capacity, and the higher are the profits which provide the finance for such investment.

Under these conditions the economic growth of particular industrial regions will largely be determined by the growth of demand for the products of those regions which emanates from *outside* the region, i.e., the growth of its exports. A faster rate of growth of exports will induce a faster rate of growth of production and an acceleration in industrial investment, and both of these will lead to a faster growth of consumption.

If the world consisted of a single industrial area which sold its products to an outside world of primary producers in exchange for food and basic materials, the growth of demand for its exports would itself be governed by the purchasing power it provided to the outside world either through its purchases of food and raw materials or through foreign investment.[2] In a world, however, where there are a number of competing industrial regions, the growth of demand for the products of *any one* of these regions will depend, not just on the growth of total demand, but on whether it is gaining or losing in competitiveness, i.e., whether it

[1] Empirical evidence derived from the comparative experience of a number of advanced industrial countries suggests that a 1 per cent increase in the rate of growth of manufacturing production requires an addition of about 0.5 per cent to the rate of growth of employment in manufacturing and will be associated with a 0.5 per cent addition to the rate of growth of non-manufacturing output. (See my paper, *Causes of the Slow Rate of Growth of the United Kingdom*, Cambridge University Press, 1966).

[2] This was largely the situation of Britain in the middle of the 19th century when she had a near-monopoly as an exporter of manufactures, and also provided the main world market for food and basic materials. The pace of industrial expansion in Britain rose and fell with exports, which in turn depended on rising or falling primary product prices— which governed the purchasing power of the producers of primary products—and the latter in turn on whether the growth of supplies of primary products ran ahead or fell behind the growth of world demand.

manages to enlarge its share in the total market, or whether it has to put up with a diminishing share.

Owing to the existence of economies of scale both comparative success and comparative failure tend to have self-reinforcing effects. Industrial areas tend to become more "competitive" when their growth of productivity is faster than average; but a higher rate of productivity growth is itself the reflection of the faster rate of growth production made possible by the gain in "competitiveness".

Myrdal coined the phrase "circular and cumulative causation"[1] to explain why the pace of economic development of the various areas of the world does not tend to a state of even balance, but on the contrary, tends to crystallise in a limited number of fast-growing areas whose success has an inhibiting effect on the development of the others. This tendency could not operate if changes in money wages were always such as to offset differences in the rates of productivity increase. This however, is not the case; for reasons that are not perhaps fully understood, the dispersion in the growth of money wages as between different industrial areas tends always to be considerably smaller than the dispersion in productivity movements.[2] It is for this reason that within a common currency area, or under a system of convertible currencies with fixed exchange rates, relatively fast-growing areas tend to acquire a cumulative competitive advantage over relatively slow-growing areas. "Efficiency wages" (money wages divided by productivity) will, in the natural course of events, tend to fall in the former, relatively to the latter—even when they tend to rise in both areas in absolute terms. Just because the differences in wage increases are not sufficient to offset the differences in productivity increases, the comparative costs of production in

---

[1] *Economic Theory and Underdeveloped Regions,* London, Duckworth, 1957.

[2] The differences in the rates of increase in money wages between industrial countries in the post-war period tended to be small relatively to differences in rates of productivity growth. In the last year or two the rate of increase in money wages accelerated very considerably in all major industrial countries, but without creating large differences in the rates of increase of wages *between* countries. Cf. OECD study *Inflation: The Present Problem,* December 1970, Table 8. For further evidence on the relation of changes in competitiveness to differences of productivity growths, see also the OECD study, "An Empirical Analysis of Competition in Export and Domestic Markets" in *OECD Economic Outlook, Occasional Studies,* December 1970.

The Lorentz Implication

policy, and in particular the level of interest rates, the method of financing the public sector deficit and the rate of growth of the money supply, and on external monetary policy, by designing a strategy in the foreign exchange markets and managing the external reserves of the Community. The local reserve banks would administer their financial systems by purchase and sale of securities, the enforcement of reserve requirements and the administration of a rediscounting mechanism. In all of these functions, there would have to be a close liaison between different local reserve banks and between local reserve banks and the federal bank. In both designing and carrying out domestic and external monetary policy, the EEC Central Bank and the Centre for Economic Policy would have to co-ordinate closely their operations.

During the first stage of the proposed transitional period for a monetary union, 1971-73, the Report sets up a specific procedure for member countries to harmonise their aggregate economic policies by applying quantitative guidelines on the principal elements of their national budgets; advocates the general intro-duction of the VAT as well as alignment of rates on both indirect taxes and on direct taxes such that fiscal differences between coun-tries do not result in capital movements within the Community; institutional and fiscal reforms which would result in a unified capital market; harmonisation of member countries' domestic monetary policies; and advocates that member countries' central banks limit the fluctuations in the rates of exchange between their own currencies to narrower margins than those which result from the present margins between their own currencies and the dollar.

Before discussing the implications of these plans in some detail, it is important to consider one particular fallacy which keeps constantly recurring at different levels of sophistication. This is, that an integrated monetary union, with a common currency, central bank, external exchange rate and a European Reserve Fund is an essential concomitant of an economic union.[1]

---

[1] "The implementation of such a (monetary) union will effect a lasting improvement in welfare in the Community and will reinforce the contribution of the Community to economic and monetary equilibrium in the world." *Report to the Council and the Commission on the realisation by stages of Economic and Monetary Union in the Community (Werner Report) Supplement to Bulletin U—1970 of the European Communities.* "If the creation of an all-European market is to have its full beneficial effects on the Western European economy, it must modify the nature, scale

The acceptance by the Six of the recommendations of the Werner Report is an inevitable development therefore for the EEC. While from the political standpoint of the EEC, a common currency may be desirable, it certainly does not follow directly from economic theory. From an economic point of view, the gain from an economic union arises from the removal of those factors which distort prices between regions or countries, such as tariffs and quotas, and which inhibit the free movement of capital and labour. This gain in real income from the introduction of free trade could arise, either from the removal of restrictions between different regions of any one country, or from those between different countries. These gains could be equally realised, whether there was a common currency as in different regions of the same country, or whether there were independent currencies and a system of flexible exchange rates between countries. The gain in economic welfare which arises from the creation of a common market could equally well be accompanied by six independent currencies which floated against the dollar, a single European currency, or, as at present, an intermediate system.

Two objections are usually raised against this proposition. The first is that if the economic gains from the common market are to be fully realised, the scale and geographical distribution of capital investment must be changed. As flexibility in the exchange rate is likely to induce uncertainty—and uncertainty such as to deter the overall level of investment—then these gains will not be completely realised. The crucial assumption underlying this argument is that flexible exchange rates would produce more uncertainty for business investment planning than would be true given a common currency. However, if we assume rigidly fixed exchange rates between countries, money wages inflexible in a downward direction and a Community-wide regional policy comparable to that pursued in the post-war period in Britain,

---

and geographical distribution of Europe's manufacturing equipment... These decisions will only be influenced if those making them are given full assurance that a free all-European market is not only established but here to stay and that intra-European economic relations will no more...be disturbed and disrupted by trade restrictions, exchange control or exchange rate revision." Tibor Scitovsky, *Economic Theory and Western European Integration*, p. 79; R. Triffin, "On the Creation of a European Reserve Fund", *Banca Nazionale del Lavoro Quarterly Review*, December 1969.

while the uncertainty of exchange rate changes is removed, a business firm making an investment decision would still be faced with uncertainty regarding the rate of regional wage inflation, the level of aggregate economic activity within the region and in particular the uncertainty as to the extent of the Community fiscal transfer, in the form of capital grants and labour subsidies, to firms operating in that region. It is by no means obvious, *a priori*, that the uncertainty from the latter arrangement would be greater than that in the former. In addition, the existence of the forward exchange market is a mechanism for combating exchange rate uncertainty.

Neither is there any reason to think that a flexible exchange rate must be a widely fluctuating rate. If some particular rate was, over a period of time, prone to substantial fluctuation, however that may be defined, then it would suggest that the cause of the fluctuation was the continual change in the underlying real economic structure, rather than simply short-term speculation. If this is true then, once again, investors would face considerable uncertainty whether there was a common currency or not. In a stable economic environment there would be no reason for widely fluctuating exchange rates.

The second objection to the existence of exchange rate changes within the EEC is the view of the Commission, "that extending the range of fluctuations of the exchange rates of the currencies of member countries would raise serious problems for the common agricultural policy."[1] The central feature of the Common Agricultural Policy (C.A.P.) is that support prices for agricultural products are fixed in terms of an EEC unit of account (equivalent to gold) and then converted at existing dollar parities into each country's particular currency. If the dollar parity of a member country is changed, then the nominal support price will be raised (lowered) by the percentage devaluation (revaluation) of the currency. In terms of the 1969 exchange rate changes within the EEC, this should have meant that the support prices of agricultural products in France increased by 11 per cent and those in Germany fell by 12 per cent.

The main effects of exchange rate changes, at least in the short

---

[1] *Approaches to Greater Flexibility of Exchange Rates. The Burgenstock Papers.* Ed. by G. N. Halm. Papers 46-49.

T. Josling, "Exchange Rate Flexibility and the Common Agricultural Policy of the EEC", *Weltwirtschaftliches Archiv,* Band 104, 1970.

run, will be transfers of income from agricultural producers to consumers at a time of revaluation and from consumers to agricultural producers at a time of devaluation. In 1969, to avoid such transfers, the internal domestic prices of French and German agricultural goods were not raised by 12 per cent and lowered by 11 per cent respectively. Instead, a process of price adjustment over a period of years was worked out.

Under the present system, changes in the exchange rate, which are as large as those of 1969, are bound to result in intolerable short-term income and capital transfers between the agricultural and industrial sectors of member countries. However, this is not an argument against exchange rate changes in themselves, but rather against the present adjustable peg system where exchange rate changes come too large and too late. If the C.A.P. is to realise its own aim of treating agriculture in each country on a uniform basis, then there must be some readjustment in nominal support prices to offset changes in the cost of living which differs between countries. Otherwise, in terms of equity, the agricultural sector of a slowly inflating country is gaining relatively to that of a faster inflating country. The objective of equity could be realised through much more gradual and possibly more frequent changes in exchange rates, which would not lead to such substantial income transfers.

The potential effects of an EEC monetary union on a country such as Britain can be most usefully discussed under the following categories : (*a*) balance-of-payments adjustment policies, (*b*) fiscal policy, (*c*) monetary policy and (*d*) the future of sterling and the sterling area.

(a) Balance-of-Payments Adjustment Policies

Any monetary arrangement, be it a system of flexible exchange rates, a single currency area or the present Bretton Woods adjustable peg system, must imply some mechanism by which balance-of-payments deficits and surpluses, either between different countries or between different regions within a single currency area, can be removed. Under a system of freely fluctuating exchange rates, the price of each country's currency in terms of each other country's currency would be determined in the foreign exchange market by the forces of supply and demand. An autonomous increase in the demand for a country's imports would automatically lead to an increased demand for foreign currency and in turn to a rise in the price of foreign currency relative to home currency. Hence, an incipient balance-of-payments deficit would be removed automatically by a fall in the exchange rate. Similarly, an increased demand for the country's exports would lead to an incipient surplus in the balance of payments and a revaluation in the exchange rate.

Under the present system, whereby the prices of currencies are fixed to the dollar and the dollar is fixed in terms of gold, a country can remove a deficit or surplus either by changing the exchange rate or the level of aggregate expenditure (which in the short run will have an effect on both the level of real output and the rate of inflation) or by imposing or relaxing controls on imports, foreign exchange, foreign investment and export subsidies. Given most countries' commitment to free trade under the rules of GATT, the two most frequent policies to remedy balance-of-payments deficits and surpluses are exchange rate changes, permitted under the IMF rules in conditions of fundamental disequilibrium, and changes in the level of domestic expenditure.

Within a single currency area, on the other hand, because it is impossible by definition to change the exchange rate between regions, adjustment occurs through changes in the level of expenditure. Whether the single currency area were a single country with a particular currency or different countries with different currencies but with rigidly fixed exchange rates, the initial impact of balance-of-payments surpluses or deficits between different regions would be reflected in their different levels of unemployment. Imagine the EEC having a common currency and an increased demand by Britain for French products. Given downward rigidity in money wage rates, this would result, *ceteris paribus,* in a decreased demand by British citizens for British products and an increased demand for French products, which would lead to a reduction in the level of unemployment and idle capacity in France and an increase in the unemployment rate in Britain. This example is exactly the same as if, under the present situation within Britain, there was an increased demand by Wales for English products. As Welsh consumers switched away from buying Welsh products, Wales would be running a balance-of-payments deficit *vis-à-vis* England. If the market mechanism were left to itself, then over time we would expect the unemployment rate to be higher in Wales than in England, leading ultimately to a migration of labour from Wales to England.

However, as this process is uncertain, both as to the extent of migration as well as its timing, most governments have developed some sort of regional policy, by which they have redistributed purchasing power towards regions in balance-of-payments deficit and away from regions of balance-of-payments surplus, mainly by encouraging firms to invest in the deficit regions through offering fiscal incentives.

By comparison with the present EEC system of separate currencies, a country belonging to a unified currency area would have no control over her exchange rate or over the level of aggregate demand, and in turn the particular choice in the short run between a combination of a particular rate of inflation and level of unemployment. Balance-of-payments adjustment policies, be they changes in the exchange rate or the level of aggregate demand, executed by a single country, are replaced within a monetary union by a regional policy for the Community as a whole, executed by some supranational Community authority.

The substitution of exchange rate changes by a regional policy is open to two serious objections. In the first place, it is virtually certain that a regional policy involving subsidies to specific industries, public investment programmes, regional premiums and investment grants which in total is as equally effective as a given exchange rate change in removing a surplus or deficit will have in addition serious side effects. E.g., a devaluation of the exchange rate would be an across-the-board change, with price changes creating specific incentives for *all* kinds of exporters and disincentives for *all* kinds of importers. On the other hand, a regional policy would almost certainly involve a distortion of market prices and rate of return to capital in various industries. While the government in the interest of society at large may rightly attempt to marginally change the composition of output by fiscal means, using fiscal policy as a substitute for exchange rate changes has an inbuilt tendency to maintain the existing structure of industry. In particular, governments have a tendency to redistribute purchasing power through subsidies to declining industries rather than by simple, straightforward fiscal transfers to those who need the money. This is evidenced in the post-war British economy by continuing subsidies to declining industries such as coal, the railways, shipbuilding and the aero-space industry which are inefficient in that they use up scarce capital resources. Secondly, the post-war evidence in Britain on the success of regional policy is hardly an encouragement for an extension of its use. Despite a vigorous attempt to aid the North East, Wales, Scotland and Ulster, the unemployment rate for these regions is substantially above that of Britain as a whole.

(b) Fiscal Policy

The Werner Report lays considerable stress on the necessity that member countries must harmonise their fiscal policies within a monetary union. It is particularly important to try to separate that degree of fiscal harmonisation which is absolutely minimal to any monetary union from that which is allegedly necessary.

In the first place, there is the extent to which the British Government's aggregate total expenditure, taxation and borrowing requirement could be independent both of the EEC budget and of the budgets of other local regions. While it is true to say that Britain would not be able to spend by creating extra money, as this would be tantamount to taxing other members of the Community, it is not at all clear that she would not be able to engage in deficit expenditure financed by borrowing on the capital market. During the last decade within Britain, largely as a result of local authorities being allowed considerable independence, the local authority capital market has grown enormously, enabling local authorities to finance various expenditures quite independently of the expenditure and borrowings of the central government as a whole. To the extent that Britain as a region within the Community would be able to do likewise there would seem to be no particular need to harmonise regional expenditure and borrowing policies. The main virtue of such a loose federal relationship even within a monetary union would be that it would help contribute to a solution of the regional problem. Although the Community lays considerable stress on the need for harmonisation of almost every conceivable fiscal instrument, there would seem to be no need either from an *a priori* basis or from the evidence of autonomy in federal states and of local authorities in such countries as Canada and the U.S.A. to harmonise local regional expenditure financed by bond issues.

Secondly, there is the harmonisation of various rates of taxation. The Report recognises that in this field there is no necessity for complete harmonisation. While stating that there should be a "progressive and complete suppression of fiscal frontiers in the

Community"[1] this should be done "respecting the elasticity that is necessary in order that fiscal policy may have its effect at different levels."[2] In particular it argues for a general VAT, alignment of excise duties that have a direct bearing on the free movement of goods across frontiers, and the standardisation of taxes on corporations and on interest payments on fixed interest securities and dividends. In broad terms the tax system for companies and capital will have to be completely standardised to avoid the creation of capital and corporate tax havens. The levels of indirect taxes could vary between regions, much as they do at present between local states within federal systems such as Canada and the U.S., up to the point where the differential between different tax rates was not so large that it would pay, after transport costs, to buy the particular goods from another country. While rates of personal income tax could also vary from region to region, the existence of differentials would be a stimulus for labour to migrate from one region to another, as well as for individuals to pay tax in the region with the lowest rate of tax and live in those areas with the highest level of government benefits.

(c) Monetary Policy

Throughout the post-war period there has neither been a continuing set of objectives nor techniques to British monetary policy. However, in broad terms, British monetary policy has attempted to control the level of interest rates, the stock of money and the allocation of credit between the public and private sectors and within the private sector to various sectors. To achieve these ends the Bank of England has set the level of Bank Rate (the rediscount rate), and depending on one's judgement, either the stock of high-powered money or the level of market interest rates. It has effectively determined the cash and liquid asset ratios of the clearing banks, the proportion of bank assets which should be allocated to the private sector, and, through the system of priorities, has attempted to channel funds into investment and out of consumption and imports.

How would these be changed if Britain were a member of a monetary union? In the first place Britain would have no control over the growth rate of the money stock or the level of interest

[1] *Werner Report*, p. 19.
[2] *Werner Report*, p. 19.

rates, this power now having been transferred to a supranational Community central bank, which fixed both the total growth of the money stock within the Community, the level of Bank Rate for the Community as a whole and if it is so desired, influenced the level of short term interest rates. The consequence of Britain being able to control the growth of its own money stock would be, that if the money stock increased at a faster rate than that of the Community as a whole, Britain would be able to purchase the goods of other member countries and so would be in continual deficit to them. Similarly, by setting the level of interest rates higher than that in the Community as a whole, it would attract funds which could be used to finance its expenditure on the current goods and services produced in other member countries. To the extent that at present monetary policy can be used to control aggregate demand, this would have to be relinquished.

It might be argued that under the present system Britain has very little independence in any case over the quantitative monetary policy it can pursue. For an open economy with a fixed exchange rate an increase (decrease) in the level of domestic credit would lead to an increase (decrease) in expenditure and in turn to a balance of payments deficit (surplus). This argument is perfectly true if the present exchange rate remains unchanged. To the extent that the British monetary authorities are reluctant to vary the exchange rate, then it follows that we have already lost our independence in controlling the domestic stock of money. In this case entry into the EEC would perform the valuable service of so clearly demonstrating how much we tie our hands behind our backs as a nation when we voluntarily stake ourselves to the existing dollar value of the pound.

Secondly, it is highly unlikely that the Bank of England or Treasury would be able to impose specific requirements on the banks such as cash and liquid assets ratios, special deposit requirements and advances ceilings which were different from those of the Community as a whole. As short-term capital is highly responsive to interest rate differentials, measures such as these, which are an implied form of taxation, would affect the rates which banks could pay on deposits, and would mean that the public would switch deposits from the British banks to banks in other countries which were not so discriminated against by their monetary authorities. Similarly, the British authorities would not be able to impose interest rate ceilings on deposits, such as they at present do by setting the level of Bank Rate, without creating short-run capital movements between member countries, and creating a Euro-sterling market comparable to the Euro-dollar market.

(d) The Future of Sterling and the Sterling Area

The creation of an EEC monetary union, as we have seen, would necessitate that the central monetary institutions of the EEC should take over and manage the gold and foreign exchange reserves of the Community as a whole. At the same time the external liabilities of each country would become the external liabilities of the Community, denominated in terms of an EEC unit of account. For Britain, this would mean that our gold and foreign exchange reserves would be transferred from the Exchange Equalisation Account to a European Reserve Fund, managed by the EEC Central Bank. However, one real problem that would occur for Britain would be the arrangements with respect to the large outstanding short-term sterling liabilities, including the sterling balances. In September 1970 the total of sterling liabilities outstanding to all foreigners was approximately £6,375 million of which the sterling balances comprise £2,597 million.[1] These latter balances approximate the extent of sterling's current role as a reserve currency. As a trading currency sterling has largely been superseded by the dollar, except in the Overseas Sterling Area. As a result of the Basle Agreement of September 1968,[2] Britain has guaranteed to maintain the dollar value of the official sterling reserves of sterling-area countries, except for a portion equal to 10 per cent of each country's total reserves. Their value is therefore protected from any future devaluation of the pound. The *quid pro quo* on the part of the holders of sterling for this guarantee in the value of their sterling was that each country maintained a Minimum Sterling proportion in its reserves, the proportion being negotiated between the individual country and Britain. These arrangements were to last three years, with a provision for extension for a further two years by mutual agreement. With the Werner Report on monetary union coming out so clearly for a common currency, the design of

[1] See "A Revised Presentation of External Liabilities and Claims in Sterling", *Bank of England Quarterly Bulletin*, December 1970.

[2] *The Basle Facility and the Sterling Area*, Cmnd. 3787, HMSO, October 1968.

a long-run solution to the future of sterling is something that is forced upon us as a result of our application to join the EEC.

To the extent that we accept the basis of the Werner Plan for monetary union, the only viable solution to end the reserve role of sterling would be a funding of the sterling balances either within the Six or through the IMF as a whole. In his proposal for the creation of a European Reserve Fund, Triffin suggests that the Overseas Sterling Area countries should be invited to deposit with the European Reserve Fund the sterling balances which they deemed surplus to their inventory of reserves to meet the needs of trade (estimated at about £8 billion), for which they would receive a deposit in EEC units of account, and which they could use to finance their deficits but not to accumulate gold or third country currencies. At the same time, Britain would deposit with the European Reserve Fund long-term bonds, which by being expressed in EEC units of account would be given a dollar guarantee. On the other hand, the sterling balances could be funded via the IMF, the difference being that in one case we would be annually transferring a certain amount of purchasing power (the annual interest and repayment) to the EEC, whereas in the other case it would be to a wider group of countries.

CONCLUSIONS

1. An EEC monetary union is *neither* a logical economic consequence of an EEC customs union *nor* an essential facet of a fully integrated economic union. It would be perfectly feasible to have a fully integrated economic union accompanied by either a regime of flexible exchange rates or the present adjustable peg system in which parities are changed infrequently.

2. An EEC monetary union as envisaged in the Werner Report and as stated in the Council's February resolution is a *de facto* political union. As such it would involve the transference of the determination of the main aspects of British economic policy from Britain to the EEC as a whole. This would mean that the autonomy which this country has with respect to the rate of inflation, the level of unemployment and the extent of regional redistribution of income as goals of economic policy would be surrendered to the EEC as a whole.

3. The main economic issue raised by the Werner Plan is the

extent to which a Community-wide regional policy is an effective substitute for exchange rate changes as a way of removing balance-of-payments deficits and surplus. The relative lack of success of regional policies in the developed countries, as well as the need for all countries with persistent balance-of-payments deficits to devalue, cannot but raise serious doubts about throwing the entire burden of adjustment on to regional policies.

POSTSCRIPT

Since May 10th and as a result of the international currency crisis both the German mark and the Dutch guilder have floated against the dollar. The reason for speculation in favour of the D-mark was the inevitability of a German revaluation, in view of the relatively low rate of inflation in Germany and the determination of the government to continue this policy. In the light of the Six's February decision on monetary union, the decision of Holland and Germany to float has extremely important consequences. Firstly the February decision is not only all things to all men, but will be unilaterally broken when it conflicts with a country's own interests. The reason the mark is at present floating is not any such nonsense as "the sprawling monster of the Euro-dollar market" but a conscious decision by Germany to aim at a lower rate of inflation than other EEC countries. Thus the choice for the EEC is between a monetary union and a Community decision on the appropriate rate of inflation or else a system of independent currencies and greater national autonomy. Present experience suggests that national preferences are sufficiently strong and diverse to ensure that, even if the facade of monetary union is maintained, countries will continue to pursue mutually inconsistent policies. Secondly, the present adjustments indicate the difficulties inherent in a transitional process extended over a number of years. The crux of this process is that countries harmonise *both* the instruments *and* objectives of policy *simultaneously*. If, as one suspects will happen, countries find it easier to agree on techniques of implementing policies rather than on the objectives of those policies the transitional process will result both in undesirable income transfers from exchange rate changes, and, because of uncertainty over the rates themselves, an even greater growth in the role of the dollar in the world economy.

May 20th, 1971

VI

POLITICAL HOPES AND POLITICAL REALITIES

by *William Pickles*

Reader in Political Science,
University of London.

W HEN THE MODERN argument began about the "creation
of Europe" and the desirability or otherwise of a "united" or
"integrated" Europe, the supporters of European "integration"
put most of their emphasis on what they saw as the political
reasons for seeking unity. During World War II, some of the
underground resistance papers, especially in France, had had
articles on the need for a larger tariff-free market for European
engineering and motor-car industries, but the main emphasis
even then was on politics. At the so-called "Congress of Europe"
at The Hague in May 1948, M. Paul Reynaud, a former French
Prime Minister, proposed the immediate drafting of a European
Constitution and European electoral law, leading to a complete
European federation within eight months. The resultant creation
soon afterwards of the Council of Europe represented a compromise between many groups—the more and the less impatient
federalists, the functionalists, the pragmatists and the sceptical
British. When it became clear that the Council of Europe could
and would get nowhere (nobody then expected from it anything
as useful as its Human Rights Tribunal), the Coal-Steel Pool was
set up, as the first move in a functionalist approach to political
union. The European Economic Community had the same
purpose, as did all the abortive projects that filled the years
between 1950 and 1956—the Transport Pool, the Agricultural
Pool, the European Defence Community and the European
Political Community.

When British membership of the EEC was first considered by
a British Government, in 1961, Mr Macmillan and his fellow

converts put all their public emphasis on the reputed economic advantages of membership, as did Mr Wilson when he in turn changed his line in 1966. Most other politicians followed their example, and only a minority of them, with a little academic support, actively preached either federalism or some other form of "integration" falling short of federalism (for which none of them has ever suggested any institutional structure). The argument of this minority has always been that nation-States of the size even of the biggest European countries (except Russia) are incapable of fulfilling the duties explicitly or implicitly expected of nation-State machines, and in particular are incapable of defending themselves against either the existing economic pressures or possible military threats from the two superpowers. The argument even of the federalists, however, and still more of the "integrationists", has always been presented in national and often in nationalist terms. Just as the peoples of each of the six member States of the European Communities were promised greater security, greater prosperity and a greater influence in world affairs *for themselves* if they federated or "integrated" themselves with others, so the British were told that membership of the Communities, followed by further steps to political unity, would give to them—the British—"a louder voice" and a greater influence in world affairs.

By the time the third British attempt at membership had begun, however, first under Mr Wilson and then under Mr Heath, knowledge of the economic problems of the Community countries had begun to spread. Though the press was in majority anxious to conceal the difficulties of life within the Community, even something less than a reasonable minimum of factual reporting had made its readers aware of the high cost of living in the Community, of high food prices in particular, of the absurdities of an agricultural policy that no British politician was prepared to defend, and of economic crises in Community countries that bore a strange resemblance to those that Community life was supposed to prevent. It was probably this greater awareness of the great difference between economic reality within the Community and the pictures that had been drawn by British advocates of membership that led the pro-membership propagandists in Britain to change their tune. What were once presented as economic advantages great enough to be worth a certain political risk suddenly became great political advantages, well worth a high economic price. The purpose of this chapter is to consider these suddenly re-discovered political advantages in the light of known political realities. What kind of institutional structure is capable of giving these advantages? What are the prospects of its coming into being? And if it does come into being, what is the likelihood of its providing the desired advantages? As has been said, there have been and still are, both in Britain and within the Community countries, two notions of the type of political structure required. Some see it as a federation, along the lines of the United States. Others see it as something less centralised than a federation, but more than a mere combination of military alliance and customs union. Let us consider these two notions in turn.

Most of the recent attempts at creating federations have either failed or run into difficulties so great as to make their future uncertain. The Mali federation, the United Arab Republic, the Central African Federation, the Ghana-Guinea Union, the West Indian Federation were all either still-born or collapsed within a very short time. The Indian Federation is under heavy strain, the Nigerian Federation led to a cruel civil war, and its viability is still doubted by many authorities. Only the older federations, established in each case in political and economic circumstances quite different from those of today, seem likely to survive, and some have doubts even about them.

There is no part of the world in which an attempt at federation would encounter as many and as profound difficulties as those that face Western Europe. The six member countries of the present Communities and the four candidate countries all have highly developed economies, each with its own distinctive features. All have different social, and political traditions acquired in some cases over many centuries, and involving unconscious habits of thought so deeply rooted that they can change only slowly, if at all. Each has entrenched vested interests determined to defend themselves. Between them, they have seven different languages. The experience of the six existing members of the European Communities, their hesitations and prolonged arguments, the rivalries of the bigger ones and the fears and suspicions of the smaller—all these exemplify the kinds of difficulty that can only be multiplied if the six become ten. It would be unwise to assert that there never can be a European or West-European federation, but it is foolish to pretend to any certainty about it, except that, whether the attempt to create it succeeds or fails, it can only be accompanied by the kind of bitter conflict that has marked every stage of Community evolution so far.

Let us suppose, nevertheless, that at some stage a European federation comes into being. If it is to perform on the world stage the function expected of any other State; if it is to have, not merely "a louder voice" but just *any* kind of voice in world affairs, then it must have a central Government, like those of Washington, Canberra, Berne and Ottawa, and that Government must, as a minimum, have total control of foreign policy, the armed forces, currency and monetary policy. It may find it necessary to control other areas of policy too, as the U.S. federal authorities have extended their control of inter-state commerce and branched out into many other fields, but the first four mentioned are the minimum. That means that, if Britain becomes part of a federation, there will be *no* British voice, loud or soft, on the world stage, no British Ambassadors or representatives at the United Nations or even British consuls, no British Foreign Secretary or foreign policy at all, any more than there will be German or French officials and policies of the same kind, and the same will be true in the other three fields. Individuals and groups in Britain will have a share—a fifth at most, if representation is proportional to population—in the making of decisions, but there will not be at any point any identifiable influence of Britain as such in the fields of activity of the federal authority. Some supporters of British membership of the European Communities honestly and publicly accept that fact. They believe, as they are entitled to believe, that the interests and aspirations of the citizens of this country will be better served as constituent elements of a larger federal body, and they make no pretence of there being even a possibility of "a greater British influence" or "a louder British voice". But they are few, and the majority of their co-propagandists either believe or pretend to believe that we can both have our British cake and surrender it to "Europe".

There is also one weakness in the case even of the honest federalists. They assume that the "louder voice" of their federal Europe will say the things that they and most of their fellow countrymen would want it to say. Having first dreamed up a federation coming into being rapidly enough to contribute to the solution of the problems they want to see solved, they then dream into the policies of the federation the kinds of solution they hope to see applied. And again, nobody can assert with certainty that they will be proved wrong. But it is not easy to see the grounds for their belief.

Look at the records of our main prospective partners. The French conception of democracy is profoundly different from ours, having grown from the ideas of Rousseau instead of those of Locke; France made no attempt at democracy until 1789 and since then she has tried and failed over and over again to satisfy herself that she had found institutions capable of translating her conception of democracy into practice—when, that is, her people were not meekly following a Robespierre, a Napoleon or a Pétain. Italy and Germany have existed as States only since 1870, and the main feature of their record since then has been the invention of Fascism and Nazism. Both have rulers who are trying hard and sincerely to give their democracies solid foundations, but none of these is foolish enough to believe that the job is finished. Spain and Portugal have applied for membership, and must get it some day if the notion of a West European federation is to have any meaning. We all know how much zeal for democracy they would bring with them. The Dutch, Danes and Norwegians are sturdy democrats, while Belgium has a mixed record. But even these four, together with Britain, would make up only about two fifths of a ten-nation federation. As for the theory, often met with, that the mere presence of Britain would convert the rest to democratic ways of life and thought, it assumes either that we have some secret recipe for democracy that so far we have selfishly kept to ourselves, or that we can transmit immunities as microbes are said to do, merely by mixing with others. The truth is that even where we have actually tried to inculcate democratic attitudes, as in Northern Ireland and elsewhere, we have had at best a very limited success. Only an incurable optimist can feel reasonably certain that a federal "Europe" would be a democracy.

It is, moreover, not only the democracy of an as yet non-existent federation that is in doubt, but also the kinds of decision the federal authorities will reach, even in the most democratic of European federations. Foreign policy, military policy, economic policy mean decisions on war and peace, the cost and use of military policy, which areas are expendable and which not, how much of our resources we spend on armaments or investments or social services, whether our monetary and currency policies are directed towards maintaining full employment, to more or less competition, growth or stability and so on. All these matters would be decided with our participation, but much more with the principles and welfare of others in view than of ours. No serious-minded individual can pretend to know in advance what kinds of policy in these areas a quarrelsome amalgam of ten nations would produce.

So much for the federalist illusions. It must be repeated, however, that in this country, only a minority of those who preach "integration" believe in the possibility of a federation. Professor J. D. B. Mitchell of Edinburgh, though he is a dedicated "European", is by no means alone in believing that "no one in modern times has made an effective federation of long-standing, *soi-disant* sovereign states. Patterns of federalism as we know them, were created for the most part against different backgrounds and for different purposes. New problems demand new solutions."[1] Professor Max Beloff, too, has opined that "it is not beyond the wit of political scientists" to devise a form of government that will give the advantages of federalism without being federal. Professor Paul Reuter, one of the French jurists who helped to draft the Treaties of Rome, went to the U.S.A. to discover what federalism was, rejected what he found, and set off in search of something different that would produce the same effect. Other eminent legal and political-science brains have now been pursuing that same search for years, but none has yet produced anything but minor variants of the system created by the Treaty of Rome.

It is still true, therefore, that the political structure of which Britain is now being asked to become a part is either something that will ultimately become a federation, or something like the present Communities, but a bit more so. It is also true that in both Britain and the present Community countries, most people hope and will strive for some half-way-house solution, evolving from the present Community structure. It is, therefore, that structure, with its possible or foreseeable future developments, that must be examined next.

That political structure today is one of the least democratic in the world, and is certainly the most bureaucratic, the clumsiest

[1] J. B. D. Mitchell, *Europe; the Politics of Pig in the Middle*, p. 2, Leeds, 1970.

and the least efficient in the world. Its major decisions are taken partly by the nominated Commission, which has the sole right to make policy proposals as well as immense powers of decision of its own in matters of detail, and partly by the Council of Ministers —one from each member country—which takes major policy decisions. The first of these bodies is in theory responsible to the European Parliament, but in practice—and by general agreement—responsible to nobody. The second is collectively responsible to nobody either in theory or in practice, though its individual members have some indirect responsibility, each to his own Parliament and electorate, *via* the national Cabinet of which he is a member. The European Parliament is a time-consuming sham, with one big theoretical power and one small real one; it can dismiss the whole Commission by a vote of no confidence, but has never had, and is never likely to have, either the desire or the courage to do so, and it has some control over that part of the Community budget (less than 5 per cent) which covers salaries and office expenses. The Community Court, which on many matters has the last word (one of its chief judges once said that it had it on *all* important matters) is well-meaning and impartial enough to please those who believe that government by judges is a desirable thing.

This ingenious but inevitably clumsy machine tries to run an industrial customs union, a cartel-and-monopolies policy, an ill defined "social" policy, a policy for free movement of capital and labour, and a "harmonised" set of taxation systems, to which it is trying to add common policies on patents, company law, rail, road and canal transport, and fuel and power. It already has a common agricultural market whose rules, if Britain and the other three applicants join, will have to suit the needs of the Norwegian farmers, for whom geographical and climatic conditions dictate some of the world's highest food prices (even higher than the monstrously high Community prices), together with those of the highly efficient cheap-food producers of Denmark, and the for-tunate fruit growers of Sicily, who grow oranges and lemons with a minimum of effort, while fitting in at the same time the unbelievably inefficient German wheat-growers, and the mixture of very efficient and totally inefficient French farmers of all kinds. Among the existing six member countries with reasonably similar climates, this system has already succeeded to an unparalleled extent in producing a remarkable combination of great unsaleable surpluses, angry consumers and discontented producers. If Britain too were to accept it, or anything like it, it would also have the effect of impoverishing some of the world's most efficient producers (who happen also to be our kinsmen in New Zealand, Australia and Canada), while raising the cost of food-stuffs at home to a level it has never reached in relation to wages since the repeal of the corn laws nearly 130 years ago. Nothing in the behaviour of the Community's political machine so far suggests that it is capable, either of performing the impossible planning task that a ten-nation community would set for it, or of coping with the social and political problems that its in-built anomalies and injustices would produce.

Indeed, the most striking feature of that machine so far has been its inability to solve the problems which even a six-member Community had set for itself. The Community was ahead of its own schedule as regards the creation of a customs union, but fell behind its time-table for reaching agreements on cartels and monopolies, social security of migrant workers, the agricultural common market, and free movement of labour and capital. On all the other goals laid down in the Treaty of Rome, years of argument have not yet brought agreement, and the same is true of other matters not specified in the treaty, but on which agreement is now regarded as essential to the functioning of the Community. These two latter groups include matters as impor-tant as a common agricultural policy (going far beyond a common market); harmonised taxation; patent and company law; common currency and economic policies; fuel and power; telecommunication and air-transport policies; and some others. On the problem of common defence and foreign policies, agree-ment is, as we shall see, far beyond the most distant horizon.

The reasons for this snail's pace, so disappointing to the enthusiastic "Europeans", are the recovery of national as opposed to European feeling, the discovery of great and genuine differ-ences of interests and habits, the disappearance of many of the hopes and fears that fed "European" feeling in the 1940s and 1950s, and—most of all—the machinery itself of Community government, constructed partly to defend national interests and partly in the belief that conflict could be made into a motor mechanism, each solution of a problem creating new problems that would themselves drive the member States into closer inte-gration, as solutions were sought for them in turn.

That theory has worked less and less well as the Community moved towards more vital areas of decision. The inherent conflict between the wishes of the nominated, bureaucratic Commission and the national interests, defended as a matter of duty by each member of the Council of Ministers, has led to interminable argument and delay—the situation described by a prominent Community official as one in which "each and every decision is a victory", merely because it *is* a decision. That is what has happened in a Community of six relatively like-minded countries. What then will happen in a Community of ten, in which interests and habits will be much more widely divergent? It is at least possible that the present "dead slow" will become "dead stop".

The prospects for democracy within any conceivable modification of the present structure are even more remote. The idea of giving real powers of democratic control to the European Parliament, without going as far as federation, has often been discussed, but has been and must remain a non-starter, partly because none of the member States is willing to make the necessary surrender of its powers, but still more because the basic nature of the Community structure makes any such control impossible. Decision making is shared between the Commission and the Council in the manner outlined on p. 115. The Parliament has always recognised that any attempt to subject the Commission to effective control would impede the working of the Communities' most essential organs, and none of the Ministers who make up the Council can be responsible both to a Community Parliament in Strasbourg and to a national Parliament back home : no man can serve two masters. A democratic structure is possible only if the Community turns itself into a federation, with a single, central, representative assembly controlling a single central Government, and so raises the problems discussed earlier in this chapter.

Some supporters of British membership argue that these disadvantages would be outweighed by the advantages of belonging to a more "dynamic" economy. That argument is answered in other chapters of this book. Others see as compensation the familiar "louder voice" in the councils of the world. In this non-federal context, however, the "louder voice" thesis is not merely of doubtful credibility; it is total, self-contradictory nonsense. It is, of course, true that *if* membership makes Britain economically stronger, then—other things being equal, which may or may not be the case—she will have correspondingly greater influence. But the "louder voice" argument is more normally found in a political, not an economic, context. It puts the same claims as the federalists—that *Europe* will have a louder voice, from which Britain will benefit. In fact, there is no "European voice" at all and there can be none, except within a federal structure. Six or ten Foreign Ministers or heads of State, meeting at intervals and agreeing on points of foreign policy only when their national interests converge, which is the most that can be expected outside a federation, do not add up to a consistent "voice" of any kind. Except on one occasion (during the negotiations on the Kennedy round, which dealt with one of the few things the Six have in common, namely, tariff levels), the six member countries of the Communities have been at loggerheads on every major item of foreign policy in recent years—Atlantic defence, Middle East, Vietnam, Spain, China, what you will, and they have only recently come precariously closer to each other on policy towards Russia and her European satellites.

Nor was anything else to be expected. As has already been said, each went into the Communities because it was persuaded that membership would help it in the pursuit of its own national interest. That is why the member States had the long battles we have read about over cartel-and-monopoly policy and agriculture before they reached agreement, and why they have failed to agree on the many other areas of policy listed above. It is why in 1953 the six Governments hastily buried the draft Constitution (which they had themselves commissioned) for a European Political Community and after 1958 rejected in succession three much milder plans for political union. It is why the present six-monthly meetings of Foreign Ministers commit no member State to anything, since in this matter, as in all the many others in which the Treaty of Rome does not provide otherwise, every member has a right of veto. In brief, and in the words of two of Britain's most prominent pro-Community and pro-membership propagandists, "the present members have failed to solve the problem of effective integration ... The national governments ... have failed to take bold enough steps to develop the range of common economic policies that are now needed, or to develop a common posture on more political issues, such as defence and foreign policy ... In the Community today, *its members have the worst of both worlds*: a more remote and less democratic form of government without effective common action." The italics are mine. The words are those of Messrs Pinder and Pryce in *Europe after de Gaulle* (Penguin Special, pp. 52-54. See also p. 162.)

It is a mistake to believe, as many British newspapers try to lead us to believe, by writing of "majority voting" in the Council of Ministers, that this state of affairs is being corrected and some sort of European democracy is emerging. The Treaty of Rome provides for *no* normal majority voting in that body except on a few unimportant matters, and even the "qualified majority", which means a two-nation instead of a one-nation veto, is used, even in cases where the Treaty allows it, only in minor matters, or when some Government wants to be able to pursue an unpopular policy and agrees to qualified-majority voting in order to be able to blame the consequences on the Community. That is because all the member Governments know that neither they nor their peoples are ready to give up the use of the veto in defence of what they see as vital national interests. There are still six national Governments, each in practice partly sovereign in matters provided for in the Treaty and wholly sovereign, in both theory and practice, in all the many matters left out of the Treaty. All have used the veto to block and delay, and all will use it again. If ever the member countries are ready to abandon their vetoes and semi-vetoes they will be ready for a federation, with the problems and difficulties discussed above. Unless and until they are so ready, there will be no "Europe" no "European voice" and none of the advantages attributed to those two dreams.

We are left, therefore, with the following situation. A federation is unlikely to be achieved in time to deal with any of today's problems and can probably not be achieved at all. If it is achieved, it will take Britain right off the world stage, will probably produce results unsatisfactory in one way or another to every political group in England, and will certainly reduce the influence of Wales, Scotland and Northern Ireland to zero. The only alternative to federation would take us further from democracy, further from the point of decision, make government slower and less efficient, multiply our conflicts with our neighbours and fail to provide either a "louder British voice" or a "European voice" of any kind, loud or soft. There is, therefore, a very real danger that, as the doctrinaire federalists hope, the Governments and peoples of the member States of the Communities, desperately seeking to escape their present difficulties, will jump from the "integrationist" frying pan into the federalist fire and end by having destroyed their countries, without having put anything acceptable or workable in their place.

There is also a further objection, which in the long run is probably the most serious of all. It is that, however worthy all the "European" projects may have seemed in the period of their being worked out, from 1948 to 1956, the change in the scale of international problems since that period has made them irrelevant to anything worth while. Neither a purely European technology nor a purely European defence system, even if they came into being tomorrow, would have any chance of catching up the vast distances that now separate them from American technology and American military capacity. The hare and the tortoise made good material for a fable, but the end of the story would have been very different if at the beginning of the race the hare had had a start of several decades and the tortoise had not yet been born. More important still, the scale of the world's major problems is too great for them to be solved, not only by an as yet non-existent Europe, but even by either or both of the existing superpowers. The struggles to avoid a disastrous colour conflict, to narrow the growing gap between the overfed peoples of the North and the hungry millions of the southern part of the world's land mass, the taming of nuclear power and of the even more ghastly weapons now being produced, the endlessly destructive conflicts in South East Asia and the Middle East, the problems of pollution and of the giant international companies that now control so much of the world's productive resources—none of these can be touched by action on a purely continental—still less a semi-continental—scale. All need action on a world scale, and if Britain is looking for fields in which to exercise her energies and her diplomatic skills, it is there, rather than in the pursuit of the useless and dangerous European chimaera, that they are needed. When shall we wake up to the fact that we are now no longer living in the forties and fifties, when the European dream seemed plausible, but many light-years later, in the seventies?

SELECT BIBLIOGRAPHY

Though there now exists a great mass of literature on the European Communities, their political problems have produced less informed discussion than any other aspect, and some of what has been published is already out of date. The material is of three types: academic examination of detailed points; wholly propaganda material; and more popular works that make some attempt at objectivity. The list below includes only works in the last of these categories, and divides them in accordance with the policy preferences of their authors.

A. In favour of British membership

John Lambert, *Britain in a Federal Europe*. Chatto & Windus.

John Pinder and Roy Pryce, *Europe after de Gaulle*. Penguin.

Roger Broad and Robert Jarrett, *Community Europe*. Wolff.

J. D. B. Mitchell, *Europe; the Politics of Pig in the Middle*. Leeds University Press.

Uwe Kitzinger, *The Challenge of the Common Market*. Blackwell.

Miriam Camps, *What Kind of Europe?* R.I.I.A.-O.U.P.

Stephen Holt, *The Common Market—The Conflict of Theory and Practice*. Hamish Hamilton.

Roy Pryce, *The political future of the European Community*. Marshbank-Federal Trust.

B. Against British Membership

E. Strauss, *European Reckoning*. Allen & Unwin.

Douglas Jay, *After the Common Market*. Penguin.

W. Pickles, *Not with Europe*. Fabian Society; *Britain & Europe; How Much has Changed?* Blackwell; *The Bourbons of Europe*, in Journal of Common Market Studies, Vol. IX, No. 2.

S. C. Leslie, *The Mirage of the Common Market*. Routledge.

G. E. G. Catlin, *The Atlantic Commonwealth*. Penguin.

Of the works that come nearest to total objectivity, the best are David Calleo's *Britain's Future*. Hodder & Stoughton, and Theodore Geiger, *Transatlantic Relations in the prospect of an enlarged European Community*, British-North American Committee.

VII

THE SOCIAL CONSEQUENCES

by David Stephen

*Director of the Industrial Unit of the Runny-
mede Trust and ex-Education Officer of the
Community Relations Commission.*

. . . Out of this vicious circle for the whole of Britain comes a
special threat for those areas in the North that are already
facing difficulties. Have no doubt about it, investment will
flow abroad, and what stays here will be put where it is best
placed for the Common Market. That does not mean
Wales, Scotland, the North East or the North West of
England. The Tories abandoned these areas in the 1930s,
they abandoned them in the 1950s, and by God, they will
abandon them in the 1970s if we give them the chance.

> Danny McGarvey (Amalgamated Society
> of Boilermakers, Shipwrights,
> Blacksmiths and Structural Workers),
> speaking at the TUC, Brighton,
> September 1970.

IT HAS BECOME a commonplace that the debate on
Britain's entry to the EEC (that "great debate" a former British
Prime Minister once hoped for) has been conducted in narrow,
economistic terms. The February 1970 White Paper dealt purely
with the economic price and consequences of entry, and, taking
their cue from government, employers, unions and political
parties have argued to and fro on the "dynamic effects", the
balance-of-payments problems, the effect of the Common Agricultural Policy, and the EEC budget. Back in the early sixties it
was different. Questions were frequently raised about the effect
of entry on the Health Service, regional policy, and immigration
control. Now few "assessments" of the British position include

consideration of these factors. And at the level of the man-in-the-
street, EEC entry seems to be viewed in essentially nationalistic
terms—what will happen to the English pub, whether double-
decker buses or Christmas pudding will survive as British institutions, and so on. This essay tries to move away from these
preoccupations, and to attempt a general and long-term assessment of the effect of EEC entry on jobs, wages and regional and
local communities in this country.

It would be a mistake to believe that legalistic interpretations
of the Treaty of Rome could play more than a peripheral role in
forecasting what the basic social climate in Britain might be if we
join the Common Market. In social security and welfare policy
we would be required—under articles 117 and 118—to seek
"improvements in workers' living and working conditions" and
"close collaboration" on these matters with other member governments. Article 2 requires "continuous and balanced expansion"
of the Community, which the EEC has taken to mean, among
other things, that a Community-level regional policy is necessary
and desirable. Under article 226 member states are authorised to
take measures incompatible with the Treaty if they can justify
them as rectifying persistent and serious regional difficulties. The
articles requiring free movement of labour (Nos. 48 and 49) have
rather more obvious and measurable consequences. But government policies, British attitudes and EEC attitudes would be
crucial within this somewhat vague framework.

British attitudes to social policy combine a general acceptance
of the welfare state with a belief (articulated by ministers of both
Governments in recent years) that "sponging" and spoon-feeding
are not merely undesirable but also wide-spread. Beliefs about
"penal levels of taxation" are currently evoked as explanations
for the poor performance of British industry. Help to the regions
is massive, and universally thought to be progressive and a fine
example of dynamic interventionism. Politicians articulate substantial fears in a segment of the population that a coloured
minority of under 2 per cent of the population is in itself a threat
to the British way of life and to the social fabric of this country.
Despite the fact that the share of public expenditure in GNP is
lower in Britain than in Germany, France, Sweden, Holland,
Norway and Austria, governments are continually urged to cut
public expenditure. In sum, to quote C. A. R. Crosland's *A
Social Democratic Britain*, (Fabian Tract 404, January 1971) "A

Protestant country, and the first to embrace capitalism, we retain a tradition (though now weakened) of self-help and individualism, of free enterprise and Manchester Liberalism, and hence of antipathy to government or civic action and collective welfare." We also retain, perhaps from the Beveridge era, a firm conviction that such welfare policies as we have are invariably lavish and altogether exceptional.

Attitudes, beliefs and ideologies in the EEC too are evolving. Uwe Kitzinger has pointed out (*New Society,* August 13th, 1970) that "until 1963 the vision of Europe was apocalyptic . . . a new heaven . . . ", while "from de Gaulle's veto of 1963 until 1969 the Community gradually sank into miserable political stagnation". Now, to judge from Kitzinger, the EEC manages its internal affairs in an essentially pragmatic way. The authors of the Treaty of Rome clearly thought that social progress was an automatic concomitant of economic progress; as a result, very little progress has been made, for example, in unifying social security systems in the Six. The free-trade dogmatism of the Rome Treaty, as well as the doctrinaire Europeanism of the early days, has tended to evaporate. Technocratic pragmatism, tempered, since the shock of the 1968 Paris riots and the disillusionment of youth, by a measure of social concern, appears to be the order of the day.

Against this background of EEC and British policies and preoccupations, we might perhaps consider in some detail British regional policies. At the level of the man-in-the-street (or in the employment exchange) the fact that Labour's massive diversion of funds into the regions was appreciated as a policy to create or safeguard jobs was revealed by the results of the 1970 General Election, when Labour did best in the Development Areas, and remarkably well in some parts of Northern England and Scotland. Peter Shore, then Secretary of State for Economic Affairs, told the 1968 Labour Party conference that the object of Labour policy was, first and foremost, to end unemployment. But he also added that "the waste of economic capital which is involved in the run-down of social capital in large parts of the country, while people are forced to migrate to the overcrowded areas . . . does not make sense from the point of view of getting the best out of our economic resources".

Peter Shore was, in fact, re-stating the essential objectives of British regional policies first laid down in 1940 by the Barlow Commission on the Distribution of the Industrial Population.

Barlow made three basic recommendations: congested areas should be redeveloped, industry should be dispersed and decentralised, and industrial development should be regionally balanced. Governments have made use of four basic instruments since 1945 in attempting to further these policies: (i) the Industrial Development Certificate system which allows the Government to refuse permission to firms to build factories in congested or prosperous parts of the country; (ii) the regional employment premium system of directly subsidising jobs, and grants for training and re-training; (iii) subsidies, grants, tax-rebates and other contributions (such as rent-free factories) to the capital costs of firms setting up in or moving to the development areas; and (iv) investments in regional infrastructure. While Labour has given priority to alleviating unemployment, Conservative governments have emphasised "cost-effectiveness"; but attention to unemployment has always been a major factor.

"As a government," Mr Heath told Manchester Chamber of Commerce on November 27th last year, "we regard an effective regional development policy as fundamental to our economic and social strategy... But we do not consider that regional policies over the last six years have given value for money." He went on to confirm that the regional employment premium would be phased out by 1974 and that money would no longer be "lavished on indiscriminate incentives". Powers would be used under the Local Employment Acts to provide more industrial projects which would create new jobs; basic services would be improved; more effort would be made to clear dereliction.

At present, then, British regional policy still has the basic object of tackling unemployment, despite a general refurbishment of the policy in an attempt to make it more acceptable to businessmen. But old criticisms remain valid. The removal of congestion—one of the Barlow recommendations—has been almost totally neglected. R. C. Tress has pointed out (in *Three Banks Review,* No. 81, March 1969, p. 18) that "the power of the Government effectively to check the growth of South East England and the West Midlands has been severely limited by the need to accommodate and find work for the rapidly increasing population growing up there". Lind and Flockton (*Regional Policy in Britain and the Six,* Chatham House/PEP, 1970) show that while governments use the slogan "Room to Expand" to attract firms to the Development Areas, in fact the urban centres there are already highly congested, despite unemployment, while, conversely, parts of supposedly prosperous areas, such as East Anglia, which are not defined as Development Areas because they never were prosperous or industrialised and so have not shown a relative decline, really do have "room to expand". If social development has not been served in expanding regions, neither has economic or social development been helped in the declining areas. Regions have only benefited "in the sense that events would have been worse off without them" (Tress, p. 19) while the "grey" areas (those bordering on Development Areas) have suffered from the relative lack of subsidies. "A widening gap," says Tress (p. 4), "is being driven between an obsolescent doctrine and the necessary acts demanded by economic and social realities."

The EEC's view of regional policy objectives became clearer in 1968 when Hans von der Groeben, Commission member with responsibility for regional problems (in a speech to the European Parliament on May 6th) asserted that "a decisive effort to even out and adjust regional structural differences as far as possible must therefore also be made if a common economic policy is to be at all possible". In other words, the Common Market was not possible if all regions could not participate fully in it. But "it would be wrong to consider regional policy as no more than an instrument for mobilising forces to support short-term economic and monetary policy. If such were the rôle of regional policy, the authorities responsible for it would need to do little more than see to the earliest possible transfer of labour from the economically lagging rural areas to the existing industrial regions . . . but . . . neither short-term considerations nor concern to preserve the *status quo* can be meaningful criteria for economic policy."

Von der Groeben's speech marked the first fully-fledged attempt by the EEC to get to grips with the regional development implications of the Rome Treaty. There would henceforth be close co-ordination between the Commission and the governments of member states on regional policy matters, and general policy guidelines would be laid down in Brussels. A joint study of objectives and priorities would also be organised. All areas would, generally speaking, fall into one of three groups—industrialised, semi-industrialised, and agricultural regions. Different policies would be laid down for each of these main categories of region, and for different types of area within the main groupings. For example, in "promising" agricultural regions "the main task is to develop existing industries and services to create a dense network of urban service centres", while in "difficult" agricultural regions, according to von der Groeben, "the authorities will have to assess whether migration from them has already reached such proportions that the setting-up of industries, the strengthening of the infrastructure, and the modernisation of farming can no longer be expected to breathe new life into them". In such areas, tourism, parks, reservoirs, research institutes, hospitals and sanatoria might be likely developments. (See table 1.)

Table 1   PROPOSED CRITERIA FOR EEC REGIONAL CLASSIFICATIONS

	CRITERIA	
TYPE OF REGION	% of working population in agriculture	Density of population
Industrialised regions	Up to 10% 10–20%	Over 250/km^2 Over 200/km^2
Semi-industrialised regions	Up to 15% Over 15 %	Over 150/km^2 Under 150/km^2
Agricultural regions	20–30% Over 30%	Under 100/km^2 Under 100/km^2

Source: *European Community*, December 1969, p. 11.

The EEC policy for industrialised regions involves ensuring that the economy moves towards the services sector, creating a diverse industrial structure, and creating jobs for workers displaced in the same region rather than encouraging intra-regional migration. The semi-industrialised regions should have improved infrastructure, training facilities and some new industries, but about three-quarters of the new jobs created should be through the expansion of existing industries. In general, while many more jobs would need to be created, the systems national governments use to aid developing regions should be harmonised according to the three-fold regional division, and should certainly not be allowed to escalate. Particularly where transport or other considerations mean that the policy of one state impinges directly on another state, close consultations should take place.

As yet, little progress has been made with this policy, and the Six have continued to pursue their own, individual regional policies. These, according to Lind and Flockton, are similar to Britain's, though in a number of respects on a smaller scale.[1] There is a danger, say these two authors, that member states might compete among themselves for investment by offering higher and higher subsidies in their development areas, but no problems are anticipated in the short term. In the long term, however, we can expect the EEC to set up new institutions for dealing with regional policy (a European regional financing body and a permanent EEC committee have both been mooted) and to begin a more thoroughgoing programme of co-ordination. Obviously, any British government within the EEC would be able to play a full part in the evolution of new policies; but the long-term trends are clear.

British regional policy is designed to prop up declining areas, not to anticipate developments or movements; the EEC regional policy, as outlined by von der Groeben, should anticipate, and even encourage, changes in the population and the economy. British regions would be re-classified in smaller, industrialised, semi-industrialised, and agricultural units. The semi-industrialised regions would be ear-marked for new industries, and new industrial developments would no longer necessarily be banned from the industrialised regions. Some agricultural regions would be developed, others marked-out as resort and recreation areas. Internal migrations would be essentially between agricultural and semi-industrialised regions, not from all over the country to the industrialised regions. This would all involve a complete break with typical British practice in regional policy, if not with the theory.

Within this general policy framework, certain specific trends and conditions could be anticipated. Geographers have shown

[1] For example, the British Government's aid to Northern Ireland (according to the Northern Irish Government's Budget statement, May 26th, 1970) totalled £77 million in 1969-70. The Italian Government (according to *Economic Events*, No. 4-5, 1970, p. 60) through its Cassa per Il Mezzogiorno (Southern Italy Development Fund) invested 5,505 billion lire (about £3.5 million) in Southern Italy in 1969; other budget assistance and the negative contribution of emigration would also, of course, need to be taken into account.

that the peripheral areas of the present Common Market are comparatively less well-off than the more central regions, and this trend would certainly be there in an enlarged Common Market. The eastern and southern parts of Britain would do well, Scotland, the north, Northern Ireland, Wales and the South West less well. Developments of an industrial nature could be expected in parts of the South East and in East Anglia, regions near the continent and already certain to do best from the Common Agricultural Policy. Rather than bringing jobs to the workers, governments would anticipate some movements of population from, say, South Wales and the North East of England to the new expanding centres of eastern and southern England. Scotland would probably no longer be one large development area; it would be divided into the three categories. Possibly the lowland area would be "semi-industrialised", and be ear-marked for substantial re-development; in any case, a switch to increased investment in the infrastructure of such areas can be anticipated. Areas like the Highlands, North Wales, parts of Northern Ireland, Devon and Cornwall might become recreational areas. In them, attempts to modernise or prop up farming might gradually be abandoned.

Presumably, also, Northern France would benefit in the long term from Britain's membership of the Common Market as the Manchester-Milan industrial strip became more and more of a reality. But would this be at the cost of investment in Britain? This question, as the quotation with which this article was begun shows, is a key preoccupation of British trade unionists. Presumably von der Groeben's answer to this one would be that if it involved developing a semi-industrialised region (say, Normandy or Pas de Calais) it would be in order in the European context; if it meant investment *not* going, for example, to the North East of England, regional policies there would see to it that the developments were anticipated and the re-location and re-training of workers planned for. Von der Groeben repeatedly emphasised the need to balance economic "efficiency" against the social cost of bringing about such efficiency.

Obviously, the EEC's regional policy is intended to be compatible with another principle enshrined in the Treaty of Rome, the free movement of labour, which will crucially affect the future of social life in this country. Again, though, the implications of the free movement of labour clause cannot be assessed in detail simply because they would, in turn, be dependent on general economic changes whose impact it is difficult to foresee exactly. Britain took in many hundreds of thousands of immigrants (aliens and Commonwealth) during the period 1948-68, not simply because they came, but also because there were jobs in Britain's prosperous areas for them to come to: as Professor Maurice Peston pointed out[1] this took place against a background of unemployment in the development areas because British governments had consciously or unconsciously rejected internal migration (taking the workers to the jobs) as too costly a way of filling the unfilled vacancies in the Midlands and the South East. Commonwealth immigrants could be brought in at a lower immediate social cost. (That social cost, as we are now seeing, has *in any case* to be paid sooner or later—unless we are to tolerate a minority of second-class citizens who are themselves prepared to accept lower standards.) The EEC will require member governments to pay the social costs of internal migration before looking outside the EEC for their labour requirements. (Table 2 shows how jobs are distributed in the Six, Britain and Ireland.)

The immediate effect of Britain's subscribing to articles 48 and 49 of the Rome Treaty (implemented by regulations adopted in July 1968), would be to remove most British immigration controls over nationals of EEC member states. They could come and go freely, either to seek, or to take up, jobs, and their dependants would be free to join them once they had obtained jobs. (And, if the dependants stayed at home, the British government would take on responsibility for *their* social security.) Similarly, of course, British workers would be free to move anywhere within the EEC on the same conditions. Immigration controls on EEC nationals could only be re-imposed, with EEC permission, if the employment situation warranted it. Residence permits may be required. The self-employed and retailers, as well as businessmen in general, are not treated as "labour" and so would not have free movement under these regulations.

In practice, the effects of these policies would be (*a*) an increase in the number of executive and professional people travelling between Britain and the Continental countries to gain experience and practise languages; (*b*) a slight increase in the

[1] E. J. B. Rose and associates, *Colour and Citizenship: A Report on British Race Relations,* Chapter 31, I.R.R./Oxford, 1969.

Table 2 HOW EUROPEAN COUNTRIES COMPARE : STRUCTURE OF THE ECONOMICALLY ACTIVE POPULATION (%)

	BELGIUM (1969)	FRANCE (1968)	GERMANY (1969)	ITALY (1969)	HOLLAND (1960)	LUXEMBOURG (1966)	BRITAIN (1966)	IRELAND (1966)
Agriculture, forestry, fishing	4.9	15.4	9.6	20.8	10.7	11.1	3.1	30.8
Mining and quarrying	1.6	1.2	2.0	0.6	1.5	1.4	2.3	0.9
Manufacturing	32.4	27.0	37.8	30.0	29.9	33.7	34.8	18.5
Construction	8.0	10.0	7.8	10.5	9.7	9.2	7.8	7.8
Electricity, gas, water and sanitary services	0.8	0.9	0.8	0.9	1.1	0.6	1.7	1.1
Commerce	16.5	15.0	14.4	14.6	16.2	14.1	16.0	15.3
Transport, storage and communications	7.0	5.9	5.4	5.2	6.9	7.0	6.6	5.4
Services	25.4	22.5	21.9	15.6	23.5	22.8	27.0	19.5
Not adequately described	2.3	2.1	0.3	1.8	0.5	0.1	0.7	0.7
	100%	100%	100%	100%	100%	100%	100%	100%

Source: International Labour Office, *Year Book of Labour Statistics*, Geneva, 1970.

movement of workers, probably more out (to Germany) than in (from Italy.) That Italy no longer has vast reserves of labour can be shown by the fact that she issued 1,300 work-permits to foreigners in 1959, 4,000 in 1963 and 7,400 in 1968. Although Britain continues to recruit Italians for the hotel and catering industry, numbers of work-permits issued to Italians are declining (6,509 in 1968, 6,333 in 1969, 4,858 in 1970). W. R. Böhning points out,[1] too, that migration is governed by historical factors: there is no history of large-scale immigration from Italy into Britain as there is into France, Germany and Switzerland. Böhning goes on : "Qualitatively, Britain is short of engineering and allied trades' workers of high skill. But the bulk of Italy's

[1] *Migration Today*, No. 15, Autumn 1970, pp. 10-12.

Table 3   ENTRY OF FOREIGN WORKERS

(1) WORKERS ENTERING EEC COUNTRIES 1966-68			
	1966	1967	1968
Benelux	60,852	34,138	30,847
Germany	397,437	139,325	390,879
France	131,510	107,833	93,165
Italy	3,368	3,688	4,973

Source: EEC, 1969

(2) BRITAIN: WORK-VOUCHERS ISSUED TO COMMONWEALTH CITIZENS AND WORK-PERMITS ISSUED TO ALIENS, 1967-69			
	1967	1968	1969
Aliens	50,304	62,267	67,788
Commonwealth Citizens	4,978	4,691	4,021

Sources: Home Office Immigration Statistics; *Employment and Productivity Gazette*, March 1970.
NOTE: These figures do not include dependants and others entering for settlement and should not be regarded as *immigration* statistics.

surplus comprises building workers and agricultural workers of low skill . . . Secondly, wage rates and earnings in Germany (and Luxembourg) are far above Britain's, and the Dutch and Belgian ones are fast approaching the British level, with higher growth rates." (See Table 3.)

Reports appeared in *Der Spiegel* in January 1971 which showed that emigration from Britain to Germany is already under way. Shipyard workers are being recruited by German firms from the North East of England and from Scotland. EEC entry would, presumably, ease and facilitate, if not positively encourage, the movement of British workers to the Continent. But the difficulty of getting acceptable international standards for many trades and professions (such as engineers or boilermakers) will militate against any vast increase in labour mobility in the foreseeable future.

Another little-known effect of Britain's adoption of these regulations would be to render illegal the Safeguarding of Employment (Northern Ireland) Act, 1947, which prevents out-siders (particularly, of course, the unemployed from south of the border) from taking jobs in Northern Ireland for which people born there or with Northern Ireland background or connections are qualified. Last May, the then Prime Minister of Northern Ireland, Major Chichester-Clark, was quoted as saying "We would view with the greatest concern the uncontrolled movement of labour into Northern Ireland." The Common Market could revolutionise relations between Catholics and Protestants in the province by *de facto* abolishing the border.

Community relations in Northern Ireland, in other words, might be crucially affected. What of community relations in Great Britain, and the position of our coloured community? There are two sides to this question : the first concerns the future of Commonwealth immigration into Britain.

At present immigration controls over non-EEC nationals are matters for individual EEC countries. Under a provision of regulation 1612/68 member countries may continue to recruit workers from countries with which they have "institutional ties". This applies at present to most former colonial territories of EEC member countries; but Martinique and Guadeloupe, Reunion and French Guiana are considered as integral parts of France and their inhabitants, therefore, as EEC nationals (who would have free access to Britain). Since the tough controls introduced since 1962 are gradually having the effect of ending Commonwealth immigration into Britain, a position recognised and codified by the new 1971 Immigration Act, the question hardly arises. Commonwealth immigrants (apart from dependants of those already here) will still be kept out, both from Britain and from the EEC. But when the EEC proposals for a common policy towards immigration from third countries are put forward (and the Commission is working on them at France's instigation) Britain may find it necessary to amend the 1971 Act. In the meantime, the small but steady influx of alien workers (to do mainly menial jobs in the service sector) will presumably continue, although, in the long-term, Spanish and Italian sources will dry up and probably be replaced by North Africans or Turks.

The second point is : will the coloured Commonwealth population of Britain be free to move to Europe? Will Britain, for example, "export" her race relations problems if Pakistanis are lured on to Germany by high wages there? The signs are that "British workers" for EEC purposes (i.e., those able to move freely) will be the "U.K. patrials" as defined in the 1971 Act. All full British citizens, regardless of race, will be free to move. But only a small proportion of coloured immigrants in this country have availed themselves of their right, now circumscribed by the 1971 Act, to become full British citizens automatically by registration after five years here. So there will be legal, as well as cultural, barriers to the "exporting" of coloured British residents, and little movement is likely to occur. The key to British race relations is likely to continue to lie with the complex problems of the "inner city", a matter EEC experts are already working on.

As for the area of social policy loosely referred to as the Welfare State, the implications are more difficult to assess. On the one specific point already mentioned, we would be required to be responsible for the social security and welfare of any EEC national employed in this country and for his wife and children whether or not they came with him; and there would have to be complete interchangeability of state pension rights. We would also be required to contribute to the Social Fund of the EEC, set up to assist workers made redundant by the workings of the Common Market. This, however, remains tiny by comparison with national welfare expenditure.

Apart from these essentially administrative operations, the EEC would expect from the British Government collaboration and exchange of information on health and welfare policies with a view to upward harmonisation. What would this mean? It would mean, for a start, that any glaring imbalances, which might encourage people to move to one country or another simply to enjoy the fringe benefits, would have, in time, to be removed. In the long term, therefore, disparities in family allowances (very large in Belgium and France, very small in the U.K.), and free medicine (universal only in the U.K., elsewhere based on the insurance principle) will have to be ironed out. There will be a clash, too, between British practice in matters such as national insurance contributions (split three ways: employer/employee/state with the biggest share from the state) and the typical Continental practice (split two ways, employer/employee, with the bigger share from the employer.)

It is extremely difficult to attempt to guess how these clashes will eventually work out, simply because the review of Health and Social Security policies which Mr Heath's government is undertaking leaves the British side of the equation largely open. But it must be said that, in general, any withdrawal of exchequer participation from the health and welfare services, by moves to make them less dependent on taxes and more dependent on contributions, would be fully in accord with current EEC practice. And, conversely, any Labour Government seeking a return to a tax-supported, "universalist" welfare state *might*—although there is no constitutional impediment—find it difficult to get such a philosophy accepted in Brussels.

The point is that, while it is true that little so far has been done to integrate social security systems in the Six, they basically have more in common with each other already than with our approach. Only a minority, in theory, can be out of step. In Britain, the state participates massively, and the traditional doctrine has been that if money raised from taxes is an essential component of the welfare budget, elected governments have power to allocate their own priorities within the general field of benefits and allowances. On the Continent, the general notion is that of insurance; workers are compensated for loss of wages or work. The "fall-back" principle—the payment of supplementary benefits to prevent hardship cases when other benefits are not sufficient, the old "national assistance" concept—is not generally accepted on the Continent. But Holland has introduced a radical new National Assistance Scheme, and perhaps this is a case where the EEC will recognise that Britain's approach, though radically different, is in advance of general EEC practice and a desirable goal.

Will wages go up or down? Will they rise to cope with the certain rise in food prices? The answers are unlikely to be found by playing numbers; every figure that is given is likely to be the object of argument—why it should be adjusted upwards for welfare benefits, downwards for a paying health service, and so on. Nevertheless, we have selected three key industries (Table 4) to give a general picture of wage rates and rises in the EEC and Britain.[1] Similarly, we should not assume that, because on the face of it certain traditional British social policies are not incompatible with the Treaty of Rome, the implications are that we can carry on much as before.

This article has had to be speculative. We have tried to examine, not what polices are claimed to be doing, but what their underlying objectives and trends are. Attitudes to internal migra-

[1] A good survey of wage rates and prices was done by the TUC in *Labour*, January 1970.

Table 4.

AVERAGE HOURLY EARNINGS OF MANUAL WORKERS (MALE AND FEMALE) IN THREE SELECTED INDUSTRIES IN THE COUNTRIES OF THE EEC AND BRITAIN, CLASSIFIED IN ACCORDANCE WITH THE INDUSTRIAL CLASSIFICATION USED BY THE EEC, 1964, 1968 AND 1969.

INDUSTRY AND YEAR	GERMANY D. Marks	FRANCE Francs	ITALY Lire	NETHERLANDS Guilders	BELGIUM Francs	LUXEMBOURG Francs	BRITAIN Old Pence
Textiles							
1964 (April)	3.18	2.81	291	2.46	33.63	—	64.3
1968 (April)	3.99	3.50	380	3.54	45.37	32.90	85.2
1969 (April)	4.28	4.08	401	3.96	49.86	37.82	92.4
Printing-Publishing and allied industries							
1964	4.14	4.83	494	2.86	41.43	48.59	95.0
1968	5.72	6.30	695	3.81	60.90	61.54	127.5
1969	6.19	7.36	771	4.48	64.48	69.24	132.9
Manufacture and repair of vehicles							
1964	4.19	3.95	439	2.93	47.02	—	90.3
1968	5.31	5.05	546	3.99	61.32	45.07	118.0
1969	5.79	5.71	593	4.37	67.53	48.10	126.9

Source: Employment and Productivity Gazette, September 1970, pp. 767-75.

NOTE These figures have not been adjusted to account for social security or other benefits. It should be noted that wages (cash remuneration) represent 91% of employers' labour costs in Britain, compared with 85% in Luxembourg, 80% in Belgium and the Netherlands, 83% in the German Federal Republic, 72% in France, and 71% in Italy. (Department of Employment.)

tion—whether you take jobs to the workers or vice versa—are diametrically opposed in Whitehall and in Brussels, and it is difficult to foresee how a British government could, in the long term, avoid radical changes of policy in this matter. In welfare and social security matters, the eventual outcome will depend on policies and outlooks: the matter is more or less open. Generally speaking, a new technocratic outlook will challenge traditional

British policies. It will be hard on some, less hard on others. Hardship, like the élites, will circulate.

BIBLIOGRAPHY

Books and pamphlets other than those mentioned in the text

S. BARZANTI, *The Underdeveloped Areas within the Common Market*, Princeton, 1965.

R. C. BEEVER, *Trade Unions and Free Labour Movement in EEC*, Chatham House/PEP, London, 1969.

E. M. BUSSEY, "Organised Labour and the EEC", *Industrial Relations*, Vol. 7, No. 2, February 1968, pp. 160-70.

DOREEN COLLINS, "Towards a European Social Policy", *Journal of Common Market Studies*, Vol. V, No. 1, September 1966, pp. 26-48.

C.B.I., "Notes on EEC Labour and Regional Policy", *C.B.I. Overseas Trade Bulletin*, No. 8, April 17th, 1970.

C.B.I., *Britain in Europe: A Second Industrial Appraisal,* 1970. (2 Vols.)

EEC, *La Libre Circulation de la Main d'Oeuvre et les Marchés du Travail dans la CEE*, 1969.

H. VON DER GROEBEN, *Regional Policy in an Integrated Europe*, Community Topics 33, EEC Information Office.

Institute of Personnel Management, *The Implications of European Integration for Personnel Management,* IPM Information Report No. 6, 1970.

E. A. G. ROBINSON (ed.), *Backward Areas in Advanced Countries*, London, 1969.

TUC, *Britain and the EEC,* 1967.

TUC, *Britain and the EEC,* 1970.

S. WINCHESTER, "EEC May Open Way to Irish Unity", *The Guardian*, December 29th, 1970.

Statistics

(*a*) International Labour Office :

Year-book of Labour Statistics (published annually.)

(*b*) EEC sources :

The Common Market and the Common Man, EEC Press and Information Office, July 1970. (19 Statistical tables.)

Tableau comparatif des Régimes de Securité Sociale applicables aux pays membres de la CEE, 6th edition, EEC, July 1970.

(*c*) British Government sources :

Employment and Productivity Gazette, Vol. 78, No. 9, September 1970, pp. 767-75. (Contains comparisions of earnings of manual workers in the EEC and Britain, and British unemployment statistics.)

Abstract of Regional Statistics. (No. 6, 1970, for most British employment statistics by regions.)

PART THREE

The Global Implications

VIII

THE IMPLICATIONS FOR THE COMMONWEALTH

by Lord Greenwood of Rossendale
Former Colonial Secretary: Former Minister of Overseas Development.

T o m e t h e Commonwealth is still very real and I have no use for the cynics who talk of its progression from disillusion to dissolution. Like most of us, of course, I have an innate tendency to chauvinism; I have regarded France and Italy not as desirable political or commercial partners, but as neighbours or near-neighbours with superb cultural legacies to whom it is always a pleasure to escape. But that very chauvinism has driven me, and I think many others, to be far more outward-looking politically than would otherwise be the case. The countries of the Commonwealth, independent and still dependent, have a certain glamour about them. It is, for example, an exciting experience on the Mexican border of British Honduras to find that one is addressing a Spanish-speaking population—or in the Ile Maurice and parts of the eastern Caribbean to meet workers of mixed races who speak something approaching eighteenth-century French. And it is not unrewarding, in the Lok Sabha in Delhi, to find that English is the common tongue and that many Indian politicans can only communicate with each other in English.

The common parliamentary tradition we share with our Commonwealth partners has, it is true, been knocked about a bit in some of the African countries, and may not have survived unimpaired and immaculate in parts of Asia and the Caribbean, but the fact that India, for example, with all its stresses, has been able to sustain democracy on the Westminster pattern for nearly a quarter of a century should afford us some scope for modest pride. So too must the way in which the peoples of the Commonwealth have been able side by side to operate, not only our own legal system,

but also French and Roman-Dutch and other legal systems stemming from the history of the territories. The Commonwealth Law
Conference in January 1971 was a marked success.

But the Commonwealth changes. It is therefore good to find its
Canadian Secretary-General, Arnold Smith, declaring robustly in
his Third Report, for 1968-70, that it is naive nonsense to dismiss
the Commonwealth as an illogical grouping of nations unable to
deal with past problems, still less capable of shaping the future,
and that the art of statesmanship is to use and adapt the heritage
of the past in order to help build the kind of future we want. I
hope that that statemanship is abundant enough, and dynamic
enough—especially here in Britain—to ensure that the Commonwealth is equipped and ready to take advantage of the opportunities which are still open to it. Differences of course there must be.
But it remains true that in spite of everything it is easier to
achieve a broad measure of agreement between its thirty-one full
members (and the Associated States which resulted from my own
White Paper of December 1965) than it is to achieve any
meaningful declaration on policy from the 120 or so countries of
the United Nations.

Here in Britain we tend too much to think of the Commonwealth as a group of countries upon whom we have generously—
perhaps even patronisingly—conferred great advantages. The
truth is that we have gained as much as we have given. Culturally
and socially we have gained a great deal—and not least from our
post-war immigrants. Politically the old Empire and the new
Commonwealth have given us a chance to look far beyond our
own shores and to develop an attitude to world affairs far more
mature than that of most other countries. And the economic
gains have been immense *both*—and this is what is really of the
most immediate importance—to the independent and still dependent countries of the Commonwealth *and* to ourselves. Their
development, and our relative prosperity, have both derived in
large measure from the trading system, visible and invisible, that
we have mutually established over the past 300 years. I am
certainly not impressed by the arguments that are advanced
about the changes in that pattern to our detriment in the last
decade; those changes derive in part from a prudent anticipation
of the effects which Britain's declared intention of joining the
European Economic Community would have on their economies
if it became a reality, and in part from their response to pressure

from us. While some British firms concentrated on exports to Europe, anticipating British entry.

The Six have stated quite bluntly that we should be required to maintain with the developing countries relations identical with those now maintained with them by the Six. It is true of course that throughout, Britain has spoken of the need for "the right terms" and included in these the safeguarding of Commonwealth interests, but as the years have passed the Commonwealth interests have been narrowed down to the sugar-producing territories and the New Zealand dairy industry. That is not enough. Sir Alexander Downer, Australia's High Commissioner in London, for example, in warning the International Investment Conference held in Brussels in May 1970 of the danger of thinking merely in European terms instead of in terms of the world at large, spoke of the crucial importance of the British market for some of Australia's major export industries— wheat, meat, sugar, dairy products, canned fruits, and fresh and dried fruits. If Britain retreated inside the protective wall the Common Market has erected, whole communities in Australia would be at risk. Britain takes 70 per cent of Australia's butter exports and the loss of this market would wipe out many farms as viable units of production. We take more than half of Tasmania's apple crop. Papua-New Guinea, for whose development Australia is responsible, sends a third of its exports to Britain; it enjoys at present a 10 per cent preference on palm oil and copra and a 15 per cent preference on coconut oil—and those preferences would be replaced by damaging import duties. A modest plus would thus become a far from negligible minus.

I am not suggesting that Australia's fears about our entry into the Common Market are more serious than New Zealand's; they are indeed less serious but they are by no means insignificant. Australia's case does not seem to have attracted the same attention as New Zealand's in the negotiations.

Four-fifths of New Zealand's exports come from her sheep and dairy farms. During the war the whole of her production came to feed us in Britain and New Zealand maintained butter and meat rationing at home until 1954 in order to fulfil her obligations to us. Almost everything she earned then went to buy capital equipment and consumer goods in Britain. Now, rather more than a third of her exports still come to us—including nine-tenths of the lamb and two-fifths of the cheese we import. And in return the market for British goods and services in New Zealand is worth about £200 million a year. As Sir Denis Blundell, the New Zealand High Commissioner, pointed out in November 1970, New Zealand is a better market for us than either Russia or Japan. The consequences of our retreat into continental Europe would be disastrous to New Zealand and to whole communities there—and extremely damaging not merely to our own export trade but still more to our honour. It is hard to see why we should pay so high a price to ensure that butter and cheese costs the British housewife twice the price at which she can now buy it.

In an essay of this length it is difficult to itemise—and in some cases to quantify—the effect on all the thirty-one independent territories of the Commonwealth and on our dependencies. But it is worth looking at the remarkable analysis "Britain and the EEC" produced by the Commonwealth Producers Organisation which exists to promote the interests of primary producers overseas and the development of reciprocal trade within the Commonwealth and the Preference Area. It has a respectable lineage going back to 1916 and includes among its forty-five members the Commonwealth Development Corporation, the Australian Meat Board, the West Indies Sugar Association, the Cyprus Trade Centre, the Kenya National Farmers Union, the Mauritian Chamber of Agriculture, and the New Zealand Dairy Board. It is in essence not a specifically anti-Common Market grouping and its assessment of the effects of British entry on its members is a markedly responsible and objective one. Nevertheless its report, published in 1970, begins with a stark, but moderately worded, warning that "the assertion that Britain's entry into the European Economic Community would not seriously injure Commonwealth trade is not supported by the facts" and it paints a grim picture of the injury which would result :

New Zealand. No alternative markets now or in the foreseeable future for the large trade in butter, cheese and lamb which account for over 80 per cent of New Zealand's export earnings.

Australia. Apart from the punitive effect of the Community's duties and levies on beef, the practice whereby the levies can be varied at weekly intervals imposes a stop-go basis on the trade which is utterly incompatible with the long breeding interval in cattle raising and inhibits marketing. It has already had the effect of placing nearby suppliers at an advantage over those who are more distant.

In the case of both Australia and New Zealand, the import duties the Common Agricultural Policy requires would amount to a tariff *of over 150 per cent* on the products of highly efficient grassland farming industries.

Fresh Food. Producers of apples and pears, bananas (the Caribbean territories), citrus (Cyprus, Africa and the West Indies), would lose the preference they now enjoy and have to pay instead the Common External Tariff. They would also suffer from the physical restrictions of access which would result from Britain's acceptance of the European Economic Community's regulations for fruit. It is worth noting that the Preference Area producers look to Britain for more than half their total export earnings.

Canned Fruit. Three-quarters of imports come from the Commonwealth Preference Area and the cost—even if they came in—would increase by half, with no doubt a decline in consumption. Flourishing and efficient industries would be drastically contracted.

Wine. The effects would be disastrous for Cyprus and a set-back to Australia.

Rum. Jamaica, Barbados, Trinidad, and Guyana, would all be damaged if a *preference* of 12p a gallon was replaced by an import *duty* of £1.12 a gallon.

Other Products. Potatoes, honey, tea, coffee, cocoa, palm oil and other oil seeds, wood pulp and alumina would all be affected. So would manufactures, semi-manufactures and services (shipping and insurance), important to any country trying to diversify out of primary products.

It is clear therefore that all the Commonwealth countries would be adversely affected in varying degrees. The damage to Britain herself would be not inconsiderable and the closing, or even partial closing, of our door to Commonwealth trade would at the same time close trade doors to ourselves which are of immense importance. Of the old Commonwealth both New Zealand and Australia would be seriously injured, and any agreement to join the Common Market should contain safeguards more extensive and more continuing than those which are mentioned normally only in the context of New Zealand and the sugar-manufacturing countries. Transitional provisions for a few years would be of little use to communities (even in rich countries) whose limited ability to change to new products and to find new markets for them in a world in which protectionism could assume dangerous proportions would simply tend to phase out the dissolution of a great trading system which still exists as a monument to the foresight of those who created and nourished it.

In 1968 our own gross national product per capita was £776—small compared with the U.S.A.'s £1,824, West Germany's £1,054, and Canada's £1,322. But it was bigger than New Zealand's £737. And *much* bigger than India's £28, Pakistan's £61, Guyana's £124, Nigeria's £29, Swaziland's £69, Tanzania's £29, Botswana's £40, and Kenya's £49—a fair cross section of those countries who now sit proudly in the United Nations as independent sovereign states. Our responsibility does not end with independence; in the wise words of Lord Campbell of Eskan, "we have not only given the new nations independence : we have also given them great expectations". Those expectations mean more than development grants or technical assistance. They mean the right to achieve that self-respect which comes from being able to pay their way in the world by selling abroad the primary products or manufactures that their capacity, their resources, or their climate enable them to market. The developed world can do much—and should do more—to increase their capacity. It can do a good deal by financing steelworks or hydro-electric power or irrigation to increase their resources. But the climate will remain, and some tropical countries will depend for a long time to come on their sugar, their bananas, their palm oil, or their citrus. Wide-spread production of sugar throughout the Commonwealth, and the existence of the Commonwealth Sugar Agreement, highlight the problem of sugar but other tropical products would suffer from Britain's entry into the Common Market, even if less dramatically.

It is therefore important to remember that our overseas trade, and particularly that with the poorer Commonwealth countries, rests on two concepts. First there is our planned and controlled agricultural policy at home. Secondly, we are one of the most open markets for food and raw materials in the whole world. Raw materials come in free of import duty. Cocoa and coffee, and some other foods, come in under our Commonwealth Preference Scheme. And sugar, bananas, and citrus come in under special arrangements. To end those arrangements as part of a deal with the Six would mean that the developing countries of the Commonwealth would suffer.

Commonwealth sugar is one, and a most important one, of a number of primary products which would suffer. About three-quarters of the world's production of sugar (beet as well as cane) is consumed in protected home markets. Half of the quarter that is left is subject to special arrangements, like those under the agreement between Cuba and the Soviet Union, the United States Sugar Act, and the Commonwealth Sugar Agreement. Lord Campbell, who speaks with unequalled authority as chairman of the Commonwealth Sugar Exporters, pointed in his chairman's address last year to three conclusions : "The first is that rich countries which import at the world market prices are riding on the backs of primary producers (many of them poor developing countries) and on the backs of other rich countries which operate special arrangements. The second is that any exporting country which loses a substantial part of its special arrangements is likely to face ruin. The third is that any substantial change in a special arrangement is likely to cause chaos in the international market (as was shown when the United States stopped buying Cuban sugar in 1961)."

Such considerations make one look with apprehension at the Six's own sugar policy—that of self-sufficiency. High prices in the Common Market countries have produced surpluses which have been dumped on world markets. "Dumped" is not too severe a word to use. In February 1970 the Labour Government's White Paper "Britain and the European Communities—An Economic Assessment" showed in Table 2 on page 9 that the Common Market countries had spent £126 million on the support of sugar. Of this £55 million appears under the heading "Market Intervention"—which means support of the internal market. The remaining £77 million is shown under the heading "Export Restitutions"—a polite way of saying export subsidies.

If, without adequate safeguards, we adopted the same system the effect on countries like Mauritius, which depends on sugar for 95 per cent of its exports, would be catastrophic. And Mauritius is not alone. Guyana, the Leewards and Windwards, Fiji, British Honduras, and other Commonwealth countries would also be seriously damaged—as happened to Madagascar, Surinam and

Congo-Brazzaville. It does not need a very long memory or much sense of history to recall the widespread unrest in the West Indies arising from the collapse of sugar prices in the thirties. And in the process the comparatively cheap price the British housewife pays—4p a pound at the time I am writing—would go up by at least 50 per cent; for the price in Italy is 8p, in Belgium 7p and in France nearly 6p. A steady market at guaranteed prices for producers who have little scope for diversification would have gone. So too would a steady supply at reasonable prices for our own people. And inevitably the poverty which would result in countries already painfully poor would restrict the markets for our own manufactured exports. Moreover, the British Exchequer would have to pay handsomely to bring all this about.

It is not inconceivable that in this respect at least our negotiators at Brussels may be able to achieve some accommodation which would not be wholly discreditable. The Commonwealth Sugar Exporters are on record as saying that no effective protection can be given to them without writing into the sugar policy of an enlarged Community the essential provisions of the Commonwealth Sugar Agreement—continued forward security of outlet and price. The Commonwealth Producers Association share this view but conclude that although the problem is difficult it is not impossible. The explicit nature of Britain's immediate responsibilities under the Commonwealth Sugar Agreement are comprehensively outlined in Article 6 of that Agreement. (See Appendix.)

Lord Campbell did not overstate the case when he told a meeting of Members of Parliament in November 1970 that "Sugar will be a test of the Six's real intentions towards developing countries. This will show whether they are a wholly self-centred, inward-looking, white enclave or not". It will be apparent that my own optimism is not great. But even if all the desiderata about sugar were achieved it would not be the end of our difficulties. All the food-exporting countries of the Commonwealth are in danger in varying degrees, and I have the gravest reservations about the propriety or political wisdom of pushing them more and more into a dependence on tourism which entails heavy infrastructure expenditure, usually involves imports across the balance of payments, and tends in the long run to produce unrest among those who contrast the opulence of their visitors with their own poverty.

Would the Yaoundé Convention help those members of the Commonwealth who were admitted to association with the Community? It would certainly not help in the case of sugar because sugar is a Common Agricultural Policy commodity; that is a lesson which Madagascar learned the hard way. But Yaoundé Mark I, II or II might help those tropical products which are not in competition with Common Agricultural Policy products *if* Commonwealth countries were given the same favourable terms as the French ex-colonies—although even that would not help to protect them against subsidised European competition in non-Common Agricultural Policy commodities, or give them guaranteed prices and markets. We could perhaps get much the same terms for Commonwealth countries as France obtained for her former colonies; but many commodities and many countries would probably be excluded and there would have to be a series of extremely complicated agreements before there was adequate cover. The difficulties would be immense and although we are applicants rather than supplicants our bargaining position is much weaker than that of France when the Treaty of Rome was being drawn up. The experience of those Commonwealth countries which have sought association with the European Economic Community has not been encouraging. Nor are there any impressive signs of an improvement in the situation. At the end of November 1970 the Community decided to offer associate membership to nine independent African members of the Commonwealth[1] if Britain joined. They would be able to choose association on the lines of the Yaoundé agreement, or the Arusha agreement made last year with East African members of the Commonwealth, or simple trade agreements. The Community further announced that it was not yet prepared to offer associate membership to Lesotho, Botswana and Swaziland because of their customs union with South Africa. All the Commonwealth countries in the Indian Ocean and the Caribbean were also excluded for the time being because they are such large producers of sugar. On January 7th, 1971, however, the *Guardian* reported that the United States had protested to Britain and the Six against what was described as "the likely proliferation of special trade pacts between Europe and the developing countries in Africa, Asia and the Caribbean". The former French territories now associated with the Market

[1] The Gambia, Ghana, Kenya, Malawi, Nigeria, Sierra Leone, Tanzania, Uganda and Zambia.

have also shown a lack of enthusiasm for any increase in their number.

So far I have concentrated mainly on the economic consequences for the Commonwealth if Britain joined the EEC. Those consequences are grave but the difficulties which would come with them would be, if anything, still graver. The damage our good name would sustain in New Zealand and Australia would be immense. But politically New Zealand and Australia are of the very greatest importance. They are growing dynamic countries which have a vital role to play in maintaining the stability of the South Pacific and bridging the gulf between South East Asia and the West. Cut adrift from the traditional trading pattern they will look more and more to the United States and to Japan and a possible Pacific free trade area. Such an arrangement could return to the smaller countries some of the advantages our entry into the European Economic Community would deny them. Otherwise our retreat to Brussels would leave a dangerous political and trading vacuum in the Pacific.

Nor should we forget what may well happen in Canada. Lionel Gelber, the Canadian historian, writing in *World View* has forecast that "after Britain has merged politically with European neighbours, the Americanisation of Canada, Australia and New Zealand will proceed faster than ever". But Canada looks warily at the strength of her powerful neighbour and at the growing American control of Canada's economy. A further erosion of the Commonwealth's traditional trading system would threaten Canada's independence still further. If continentalism is good for Europe, why not for North America? Those who favour a high tariff wall round our own continent can hardly complain if the United States develops protectionist tendencies. The situation was well summarised in *The Times Business News* on November 12th, 1970 :

Protectionism Can Split World Into Trade Blocks, says Report
The world is in danger of dividing up into a group of rival and restrictive trading blocks. This warning is given in a report published today, and backed by a group of leading United Kingdom and American businessmen, which looks beyond the immediate threat of United States trade protectionism.

This danger will be increased by the expansion of the Common Market to include Britain and other applicants, unless Britain uses her influence within the Community to foster more liberal trade policies, the report says.

It calls for a series of major concerted actions by the leading industrialised countries to promote free trade and to avert "the danger of starting a vicious spiral of mutual restrictions and retaliations".

The report is sponsored by the British-North American Committee, set up in December 1969 to look at the way relationships are developing between Britain, the United States and Canada. Its co-chairmen are Lord Howick, chairman of the Commonwealth Development Corporation, and Mr Harold Sweatt, chairman of the Board of Honeywell, in the U.S.A.

Basically the resourcefulness and ingenuity of our statesmen here in Britain, in America, in Japan, in continental Europe, in the Communist Bloc, and in the developing countries, should be directed with increasing intensity towards dismantling the inward-looking protectionist groupings that the post-war years have produced. No doubt we have to engage in prolonged negotiations with the Six—the developments of the last decade probably made them inevitable—but we should meanwhile also be concerning ourselves with the alternatives.

It is not *either* Europe (i.e., Six West European members of NATO) *or* the Commonwealth. Vast areas of the world have a real interest in stopping the drift to protection. And free trade areas need not be regional in character. A near-global free trade area comprising besides ourselves our EFTA friends, those Commonwealth countries who wished to join, Japan, and the United States, would offer far better prospects to the developing countries of the Commonwealth and also to Britain herself than anything which is likely to emerge from our talks in Brussels. Far from being little Englanders those of us who fear the consequences of integration into rich white Europe are looking much further afield. And we shall need far stronger arguments than the proponents of the Common Market have so far advanced, and much more effective safeguards for a much wider range of countries and products than even the most skilled negotiators are likely to secure. Without such safeguards we cannot contemplate with equanimity the appalling damage to the Commonwealth— and to ourselves as members of the Commonwealth—which our entry into the EEC would cause.

APPENDIX

Article 6 of the Commonwealth Sugar Agreement negotiated in 1968 :

1. Subject to the following provisions of this Article the Agreement shall be of indefinite duration.

2. The Agreement shall be subject to triennial review, in discussion between the parties, to such extent as any party may desire. The first such review shall be held in 1971.

3. (*a*) Changes in the Agreement, other than those which can be mutually agreed under paragraph 6 below, shall be subject to the following periods of notice given in the course of the year of review :

(i) in respect of all provisions of the Agreement (as amended by agreement between the parties) except as detailed in sub-paragraph (ii) below : three years' notice;

(ii) in respect of Articles 4, 12 and 13[1] (as amended by agreement between the parties) in so far as they impose obligations on the less-developed Exporting Territories, and on the United Kingdom Government in regard to purchases of sugar of the quantities provided for from those Exporting Territories : six years' notice.

(*b*) The provisions of this Article are subject to the understanding that the United Kingdom Government, if it successfully completes negotiations for the accession of the United Kingdom to the European Economic Community,

(i) cannot be committed to continuing contractual obligations under the Agreement after December 31st, 1974;

(ii) shall, in the event that it does not accept such contractual obligations after December 31st, 1974, consult with the other parties to the Agreement with a view to seeking means of fulfilling the objectives which those obligations would otherwise fulfil.

4. For the purposes of the provisions of paragraph 3(*a*) of this Article the period of notice given in the course of the year of review shall be deemed to commence on January 1st in the calendar year immediately following the year of review.

[1] Articles 4, 12 and 13 provide for the supply and purchase of negotiated price quotas.

5. If in the course of any triennial review it has not been possible to reach agreement between the parties on any change in the Agreement of which the United Kingdom Government has given notice in accordance with paragraph 3(*a*) of this Article, and such notice has not been withdrawn, such changes shall have effect on the expiry of the period of notice specified in that paragraph.

6. Notwithstanding any other provision in this Article any changes in the Agreement may be agreed between the parties at any time and any such changes shall have effect from such date as may be agreed.

7. In accordance with the spirit of co-operation in which the Agreement has been and will continue to be administered, full consultation shall take place between the parties in an endeavour to reach agreement on any proposed changes in the Agreement.

BIBLIOGRAPHY

The Treaty of Rome.

Publications of the Joint Information Services of the Economic Communities including "Economic Union and Enlargement", October 1969.

Hansard Official Reports.

H.M.G. White Papers in 1963; Cmnd. 4289, "Britain and the European Communities—An Economic Assessment", February 1970; Cmnd. 4401, "The United Kingdom and the European Communities", June 1970.

LORD WALSTON, *Farm gate to Brussels,* May 1970.

LEONARD BEATON, *Commonwealth in a New Era,* June 1969.

Third Report of the Commonwealth Secretary General, December 1970.

"New Zealand and an enlarged EEC" (New Zealand Monetary and Economic Council Report), June 1970.

Monthly Bulletins of the Commonwealth Industries Association.

Commonwealth Sugar Exporters Report, Spring 1970.

"Britain and the EEC—Implications for Commonwealth Primary Producers", Commonwealth Producers' Organisation, Autumn 1970.

T. E. JOSLING, *Agriculture and Britain's Trade Policy Dilemma,* December 1970.

IX

THE IMPLICATIONS FOR THE THIRD WORLD

by David Wall

Lecturer in Economics, University of Sussex.

IN A WORLD trading environment in which many changes are currently taking place it is difficult to isolate the likely impact of any one change. It is especially difficult to estimate the likely impact of the entry of Britain into the EEC on the interests of less-developed countries—partly because it is necessary to take into account the many (both competitive and complementary) interests involved and partly because there has been no indication from either side of the negotiating table of any detailed policy position with regard to safeguarding the interests of the Third World. It is important, however, to bring the issue to the forefront of public discussion because of the special nature of Britain's relationship (through its central role in the Commonwealth) with the Third World and because of the inward-looking bias of the EEC.

One way of measuring the importance of developed countries to less-developed is to look at their importance as trade partners. Roughly 20 per cent of the total imports of the EEC come from less-developed countries compared with Britain's 26 per cent from the same sources. While 5 per cent may seem a small margin between the two percentages the absolute value of trade represented by the differences is of crucial importance to the exporting country. Thus, taking the extremes, if Britain's trade with less-developed countries were to adapt to that of the Community, it would entail a fall in her imports from them of around one billion dollars. The opposite extreme would be achieved if the Community import pattern changed to that of Britain: the Community's imports from less-developed countries would rise by over four billion dollars. The difference—about five billion dollars—is roughly equivalent to one-eighth of all industrial countries' imports from less-developed countries.

The validity of the figures quoted in the last paragraph depends on the assumption that the import patterns differ at present because of differing policy measures, which affect conditions of production and consumption, rather than differences in consumer preferences. While it would be difficult to substantiate this for every commodity there is a considerable body of evidence to suggest that the EEC's lower ratio of imports from less-developed countries reflects more restrictionist policies than prevail in Britain. Examples of this contrast abound. Thus the Community operates a sugar policy which guarantees the whole of the Community's sugar market for domestic producers, while the Commonwealth Sugar Agreement guarantees a substantial part of Britain's market for sugar to less-developed producer countries. Similarly the major member countries of the Community tax the consumption of beverages imported from the less-developed Third World; Britain does not. And of products exported by less-developed countries more enter the United Kingdom free of duty than enter the Community; and where duties are applied, those imposed by the United Kingdom are frequently lower. Finally, although both Britain and the EEC operate preferential tariff systems in favour of selected less-developed countries, more (and bigger) countries benefit, on a wider range of products, from Britain's system than do under the parallel Community system, and fewer are required to provide reciprocating concessions.

To the extent, then, that the relative trade performance of less-developed countries in the markets of Britain and the EEC can be explained by policy factors, it is obvious that these countries have an intense interest in the nature of the outcome of the current negotiations. This is especially true for the less-developed countries of the Commonwealth. And yet the negotiations are proceeding with almost no attention being given to the impact of an enlarged Community on the Third World in general and the less-developed Commonwealth in particular. All that has emerged on this score are the following statements : one, attention will be given to the interests of beneficiaries of the Commonwealth Sugar Agreement (which covers Australia as well as less-developed countries); two, British dependent territories (except for Hong Kong and Gibraltar) will be treated in the same way as overseas territories of existing members; three, some Commonwealth African countries will be allowed to apply for "association" with the Community; four, Caribbean Commonwealth countries can be expected to negotiate trade agreements for the specific products in which they are interested; and finally the problems of the Asian members of the Commonwealth will be studied during Britain's transition period to full membership of the Community. Nothing is held out for the independent less-developed countries, especially those in Latin America, other than hope for benefits from the UNCTAD-sponsored preference scheme and "spill-over" effects from the growth of Community income.

That the nature of the situation is not fully appreciated by the British Government is clearly demonstrated in Mr Rippon's statement to the House of Commons on December 10th, 1970. In this statement he said:

"We are concerned that the enlarged Community should have good trading relations with the developing countries as a whole, including the Commonwealth.

"We must be desperately concerned about the trade of all these small developing Commonwealth countries. The best way we can protect it is to ensure we are strong enough within the enlarged Community to be able to buy what they have to sell."

This statement misses the point, which is that the amount and source of imports from less-developed countries into the EEC and Britain is to a large extent determined by policy measures rather than by the economic strength of those countries. The issue now is whether or not an enlarged Community, including Britain, would increase the severity of the existing restrictions on imports from the Third World. Furthermore one must ask whether or not the process of enlarging the Community would slow down the world-wide liberalisation of trade which has been taking place since the end of the Second World War. The first signs that it might be coming to an end have been evident in the U.S. protectionist lobbies during the last year. Mr Rippon's "desperate concern" is in fact inconsistent with one of the prime objectives of the Community which is to enhance its own economic strength by increasing its self-sufficiency. This is not to say that enhanced economic strength is incompatible with increased flows of imports from underdeveloped countries, but it is hardly a prerequisite. The only overriding condition is a desire to reduce discrimination against imports from poor countries. There is little evidence at present of such a desire.

What does Mr Rippon mean by the phrase "good trading relations"? At present the members of the EEC and Britain (as a member of EFTA) collectively discriminate against imports from Third World countries (Britain and the Community favour some Third World countries over others), and impose impediments to some imports from that source. In addition, British membership of the Community would automatically worsen the trade prospects of several less-developed countries as their benefits under the Commonwealth Preference System would be abolished and not replaced by any compensating benefits. Finally, if Britain were to adopt the Community's offer of preferences under the UNCTAD[1] scheme then the value to the less-developed countries of Britain's participation in that scheme would be much reduced. Mr Rippon's phrase has a hollow ring to it.

In the absence of any definite detailed statement concerning changes an enlarged Community would make in the trade policy towards less-developed countries it is not possible to set out definitive predictions of the effects of that enlargement on the less-developed countries. All that is possible is to identify forces which are at work in any case, allowing for possible changes which have been indicated, and assess their likely impact on the Third World, broken down into groups with similar interests. The two most important policy-determined factors which are at work are the Yaoundé Convention and the UNCTAD preference schemes. The most important modifications which must be allowed for are those contained in the statements listed above concerning the less-developed members of the Commonwealth.

Groups of countries can be identified according to the degree to which they could expect preferential treatment from the expanded Community under the Yaoundé Convention (and other special arrangements) as qualified by the coming-into-operation of the UNCTAD-sponsored preference scheme. This last qualification is an important one as it could seriously reduce the value of the preferences currently extended by the Community and Britain to the members of their preference schemes. The

[1] The United Nations Conference on Trade and Development.

final outcome is uncertain as so far there has not been any indication as to whether an enlarged Community's UNCTAD preference scheme would take the form of that currently offered by the Six or that offered by Britain. In fact one of the reasons why the form of the UNCTAD scheme differs according to the country (or group) operating the scheme was the difficulty of reconciling a uniform scheme with the interests of currently preferred less-developed trading partners. As they presently stand the schemes of both the Community and Britain contain the proviso that the preferences to be implemented after ratification would to some extent depend on the outcome of negotiations with members of their existing preference schemes. In addition the British scheme includes the qualification that if less-developed Commonwealth countries who lose benefits under the present Commonwealth Preference System do not receive adequate compensatory benefits in other markets under the UNCTAD scheme then the British offer will be modified. A similar clause is contained in the Community's offer, but in this case the safeguard will be implemented through a tariff qutoa system which will limit imports preferences from those less-developed countries who do not currently benefit from special preferential trading arrangements with the Community. An, as yet, unknown factor which limits the value of these safeguards is the fact that the United States scheme includes a proviso stating that the continued operation of the United States scheme is conditional on the elimination of the special preferences implied by such safeguards.

Another, in this context, crucial difference between the two schemes is that while the offer of preferences for processed agricultural products in Britain is based on zero tariffs, that in the Community scheme is based on quite small cuts in the full tariff rate. This would frequently leave quite substantial protection (up to 34 per cent) for processing industries within the Community and in the beneficiary countries of the Community's existing preference schemes. For the most part imports of processed agricultural products from these countries enter the Community duty free.

Clearly any attempt to guess at the nature of an enlarged Community's UNCTAD preference offer is, at this stage, a matter of political judgement. There has been no official guidance on this point. It is the author's opinion, however, that the joint offer is most likely to take the form of the current

Community offer. In that case current beneficiaries of the Commonwealth Preference System not included in the special preferential arrangements of the enlarged Community under the Yaoundé Convention (mainly the Asian and Caribbean Commonwealth members) would find their traditional tariff-free protected markets for processed agricultural products in Britain closed by one of the highest tariff barriers in the world. Their only hope would be for specially negotiated trade agreements with the enlarged Community. It is unlikely that in such a situation Britain would hold out against its fellow members of the Community and the client states in French-speaking Africa to ensure that no losses are incurred by such Commonwealth countries. Indeed as the bilateral trade agreements, and all other specially negotiated arrangements, of the Community are based on substantial reciprocal concessions, such losses are virtually guaranteed.

Another group of Commonwealth countries which must almost certainly incur substantial losses following Britain's joining the Community, comprises those countries which are developing markets in Britain for manufactured goods and which would be excluded from benefits under the Yaoundé Convention. Except for textiles, there are no quantitative restrictions on imports into Britain of manufactured goods from less-developed Commonwealth countries. Such trade has in recent years contributed significantly to the economic development of several Commonwealth countries, especially among those in Asia and the Caribbean. These countries will lose their unprotected markets in Britain. The Community's UNCTAD preference scheme, which is being held up to them as compensation, will place restrictions on the total value of imports of such manufactured products as would benefit from preferences—both at the initial level of such imports and at later, expanded levels. In addition, no beneficiary of the scheme will be allowed to supply more than half the total preference quota in any year. The rigidity and arbitrariness of these rules presents the possibility of some serious anomalies arising. For example, if a beneficiary country, on the basis of the preferences, develops a competitive advantage in a specific manufactured good it will find that the value of the Community preference is dependent on the level of the Community's imports from *developed* countries *and* uncompetitive less-developed countries. This follows from the rules that no beneficiary can provide more than half the quota, and that the quota is set at a level equal to the value of the Community's imports of the product from beneficiaries in 1968, plus 5 per cent of the c.i.f. value of imports from non-beneficiary (developed) countries. The countries which obviously stand to lose considerably in that situation include India, Pakistan, Malaysia, Singapore and Hong Kong.

So far we have identified one group of countries—those Commonwealth countries who would not benefit under the Yaoundé arrangements. Their experiences would depend partly on the nature of their exports and partly on the nature of any trade agreements they may be able to negotiate with the enlarged Community. On the basis of the evidence we have to hand, however, they would almost certainly all be net losers as a result of Britain joining the Community. The losses of these countries, added to the losses of consumers in Britain, would be balanced by the gains of producers in the enlarged Community, the Community's specially preferred suppliers (not all less-developed countries), or other less-developed countries with which the Commonwealth countries would have to compete on an equal footing. It is to these last two groups of countries which we will now turn our attention, having noted in passing that domestic producers in the enlarged Community would benefit from the increased protection implied by the changes.

The first group is composed of those countries which would be associated with the enlarged Community by the Yaoundé Convention (or its replacement) and other countries with special trade links. At present the association arrangements take several forms. The French overseas departments are treated as part of the Community itself and will be more-or-less unaffected by the changes. Overseas dependencies of France and Holland are extended the same commercial policy treatment by the Community as is applied to intra-Community trade, including similar rights and obligations under the Common Agricultural Policy. The existing Associated States and the remaining British dependencies (except Hong Kong) are likely to be offered a similar arrangement. The Yaoundé Convention created a series of free trade areas between the Community and eighteen ex-colonies of the Six. Nine Commonwealth countries in Africa (the black states, except for Botswana, Lesotho, Swaziland, and South West Africa, which might be excluded because of their arrangements with South Africa) would, it has been stated, be offered the same treatment. For the East African countries and Nigeria this would be a replacement for their existing association links with the Community.

For the most part the overseas departments and dependencies are very small units and the impact of the proposed changes on them will be ignored here on the grounds that any benefits they receive would have little effect on the total markets of other countries and that any losses they incur can be regarded as grounds for compensation from their metropolitan powers. Our real concern is with those countries associated with the Community via the Yaoundé Convention, or which have been promised such association. So many at present not quantifiable factors have to be allowed for that the eventual effect upon the trade interest of these countries is difficult to assess. First, the UNCTAD preference scheme would eliminate their special preferences for manufactured products, although any interests they have in this field would be to some extent safeguarded by the tariff quota restrictions of the Community's scheme. In fact, as none of the present or proposed beneficiaries under the Convention have any significant interest in exports of manufactured products the benefits of these restrictions will probably accrue to Community producers and producers in non-Community developed countries. Secondly, the present Convention beneficiaries would have to share with their new colleagues their heavily protected market in the Community for processed agricultural products. They would receive in return free access to a newly protected British market, but since in most items they are less competitive than the Commonwealth countries in Africa they would be unlikely to make many inroads into this market and would probably stand to lose much of their market in the Community. *Prima facie* it would appear then that the market situation of the Commonwealth African countries offered Associate status would improve, largely at the expense of the present Associates. But the long-term continuance of such benefits will be in jeopardy as long as the Community and United States viewpoints on discriminatory preference schemes remain unreconciled.

The remaining group of countries to be considered comprises the non-Commonwealth countries which will not have any special access to the market of the enlarged Community except via the UNCTAD preference scheme. On the assumption, made above, that the enlarged Community's scheme would be closer in form to the offer of the Six than to that offered independently by

Britain, then the mostly trivial preferences offered on processed agricultural products can be discounted. These preferences are unlikely to have any significant effect on trade flows. For manufactured products the situation is unclear. Those countries which would benefit under the scheme and which have developed export lines in manufactured goods (mainly Taiwan, Korea, the Phillipines, Mexico and Argentina), could make a once-for-all gain to the extent of the m.f.n. tariff times the share they manage to acquire of half the Community's imports from them of the relevant products in 1968 plus 5 per cent of such imports from all sources. This gain is unlikely to have any marked effect on the total foreign exchange earnings of the countries in question. And against this gain must be set the *new* limitations imposed on the *growth* of such exports, and the expansion in the number of less-developed countries who will not be subject to such restrictions (the Commonwealth African countries).

SUMMARY AND CONCLUSIONS

The enlargement of the European Economic Community from six to ten members would create the world's largest trading bloc in which imports from all non-members would be discriminated against. In itself this represents a substantial worsening of the overall trade position of the Third World. But two other changes must also be taken into account. First, there would be an increase in the number of less-developed countries having the same trade access to the markets of Community countries as the Community's members. Secondly, there is the probability that the enlarged Community would operate an UNCTAD preference scheme along the lines of that currently being offered by the Community.

This essay has been reasoned in terms of the broad changes in commercial policy structure that would be faced by less-developed countries with export interests in the enlarged Community. Within this framework it is argued that Commonwealth countries which gained association rights within the Community would stand to benefit. But these benefits would largely be at the expense of countries who already enjoy rights of association with the Six. In addition these benefits for certain less-developed Commonwealth countries would be cancelled by the loss of special preferences in the British market. Unless concessions are made, Hong Kong in particular would find itself with a substantially worsened trade environment. It has also been argued that the UNCTAD preference system might confer some small-scale short-term benefits on some less-developed countries exporting manufactured goods, but that such benefits would be at the expense of the long-term interests of all less-developed countries. If on the foregoing evidence it is also allowed that the process of enlargement of the Community would operate to slow down the momentum of world-wide trade liberalisation then it is difficult not to reach the conclusion that the process would involve a serious threat to the trade interests of less-developed countries.

None of this is surprising if one considers that some of the world's largest, protectionist-minded countries are being allowed to dictate the terms on which they will allow imports into their markets without fear of retaliation. It is understandable that they should use their monopsonistic trading power to create the trading environment most conducive to their own interests.

In this situation the British Government has stated frankly that its negotiating position is based on the principle that British interests come first and that consideration of the interests of its trading partners in the Commonwealth and elsewhere will not impede the negotiations. What is also clear, but unstated, is that so far the British Government has given little thought to the effect its joining the Community would have on the trade interests of less-developed countries, both inside and outside the Commonwealth. No attempt has been made even to calculate the magnitude of that effect. In the circumstances Mr Rippon's phrase expressing concern can only be regarded with scepticism by the countries of the Third World.

X

THE IMPLICATIONS FOR THE WORLD ECONOMY

by Harry G. Johnson

Professor of Economics, The London School of Economics and Political Science, and the University of Chicago

IF BRITAIN SUCCEEDS in acquiring membership in the European Economic Communities, the long-term implications for the world economy will be both far-reaching and potentially ominous. First, entry will inevitably entail the break-up of the system of Commonwealth preferences, and also probably the termination of the arrangements by which Commonwealth countries have had preferential access to the British capital market; indeed, the balance-of-payments pressures on Britain which are likely to ensue on membership may induce Britain to discriminate against capital exports outside Europe as an offset to the adverse balance-of-payments effects of freedom of capital movements within Europe. Thus the Commonwealth, which in a sense has been an unheralded experiment in the promotion of economic development by preferential arrangements for developing countries with a major industrial power, will cease to play that role. Second, considering the developing countries more generally, the accession of Britain to the Common Market will mean a substantial increase in trade discrimination among them, those that are now or will later become associated with the European Economic Communities benefiting from preferential access to the European market at the expense largely of other rival developing countries. Essentially, this will mean discrimination in favour of the African countries—already more favoured in the distribution of aid money than the rest—and against the Asian and Latin American countries; and since the United States will be likely in future to accentuate its special relationship with Latin America, the prime losers are likely to be the Asian countries. Further, the substantial fiscal and balance-of-payments burden that Britain will assume in the form of its contribution to the central funds of the EEC will likely induce Britain to cut back heavily on its contributions of development assistance, thereby further worsening the development prospects of the developing countries.

These and other implications of British entry into the EEC have been explored in the preceding two essays in this section. This essay is concerned with the broader implications of British entry for the world economy as a whole. Here there are two types of questions to be considered : the objectively likely effects of British entry on patterns of world trade and investment, and the possible effects of an agreement to join the EEC on the structure of institutional rules governing international economic relations. In both contexts, there are four relevant and important aspects of entry : changes in the pattern of barriers to industrial trade, the adoption of the Common Agricultural Policy, the adoption of a common currency, and the fiscal burden on Britain of contributing to the central funds of the Community.

As regards objective probabilities, the purpose of the exercise is to obtain for Britain a preferred position in the European market, at the expense of the sacrifice of preferential positions in the Commonwealth markets and in the European Free Trade Association. (While some other members of EFTA will also join the EEC, this will mean only that they will not discriminate against British goods; Britain will still lose her preferences over continental European goods in their markets.) The result will be a shift in the patterns of British exports and imports towards trade with Continental Europe and against trade with the outside world, as a result of the complementary pressures of reciprocal free trade with Europe and the loss of preferences—and possibly the erection of further barriers—in third-party trade.

The more important question, however, is whether this shift in trade patterns will produce a rejuvenation of the British economy, and a take-off into substantially more economic growth, as the proponents of entry assert, or whether it will aggravate the forces that have hitherto held back the British growth rate and so brought about a gradual dwindling of the importance of Britain in the world economy. Most of the evidence of experience—while admittedly elusive and debatable—suggests that the result is

likely to be a further decline in the world economic importance of
Britain. For this view there are many reasons. If one envisages
Europe as eventually becoming a fully integrated economy like
the United States, Britain's position is that of an offshore island,
or a peripheral coastal region such as New England in relation to
the rest of the U.S. The costs of competing from the periphery,
over transport costs, language barriers, etc. will be substantial;
and they will be aggravated by the commitment to a common
currency, since Britain apparently has a chronic tendency to
excessive inflation, which she would no longer be able to offset
(belatedly) by devaluation of the pound. Add to this the fiscal
burdens of membership of the EEC, which will have to come out
of the standard of living of the average British citizen, and the
real costs of supporting British agriculture at the levels of prices
set by the Common Agricultural Policy, and there becomes a
strong probability that both British firms and the British working
force will begin to drift towards locations on the Continent. The
most economically-oriented of the British population have been
emigrating for over two centuries; but hitherto they have been
obliged to go a very long way, and have predominantly gone to
English-speaking countries which have retained a respect for, and
willingness to help, the mother-country. Once the idea gets
established that one can live in Europe yet remain British, flying
home for Christmas or New Year's or even for long week-ends,
or that one can live in London but conduct one's business in
Germany, France or Italy, there is likely to be a substantial shift
of industrial activity away from British towards continental
locations.

The structure of the British economy is very likely to change
markedly, as the New England economy has done, away from
industrial production towards the production of services. Within
the EEC, Britain will obviously have a comparative advantage
in the provision of financial services, by virtue of the public school
system and an effortless command of the American language. It
will also—at least until the national belief in high taxation and
equality of educational misery take their toll—have a comparative advantage in university-level education, design and research
and development. But these activities will support only a relatively
small population; and one can readily envisage a gradual coalesc-
ence of the British population into a single urban conglomera-
tion centred on London and its environs, with a decaying

hinterland exporting workers to the Continent and educated people to the London megalopolis.

An important consideration in this connection is the likely effect of British membership in the EEC on the operations of the multi-national companies. This question is usually posed in terms of the decisions of the giant American companies. The Americans, however, have merely been the obvious leaders in a general trend towards multi-nationalism, a trend which itself has merely continued a previous trend for local companies to expand into national markets. Local and national companies in Europe are in the process of expanding into European-wide and multi-national companies. The question is not really whether American companies will choose to locate themselves in Britain rather than on the Continent to serve the European market—though free trade between Britain and Europe and the prospective termination of Commonwealth preferences would tend to bias that choice towards a Continental location—but whether a European company, whatever its nationality, would choose a Continental or a British location as a base from which to serve the whole European or the world market. Aside from financial and education-intensive activities, the balance of locational advantage would seem in general to lie in favour of the Continental rather than the British location. Recent American economic history, in fact, bears witness to the strength of pressures for agglomeration of economic activities into a few major centres, each with its own range of definite comparative advantages.

The foregoing remarks pertain to the objectively likely effects of British entry into the EEC on patterns of world production, trade, and investment, on the assumption that British entry will constitute a "once-over" change in the structure of world trading relationships. It is important, however—and particularly important for British public opinion—to realise that Britain's actions have implications for the attitudes and actions of other countries, and especially for the attitudes and actions of the United States; and that these implications will influence the general climate and structure of future international economic relationships.

Throughout the period since the Second World War, there has been a conflict between two sharply opposed principles of international economic organisation, a conflict inherited from the dark days of the great economic collapse and consequential constriction of world trade of the 1930s. The one principle, enshrined in the General Agreement on Tariffs and Trade, is that of non-discrimination in international trade—equal treatment of imports from all sources—and of bargaining for reciprocal tariff reductions on a non-discriminatory basis. This has been the basic principle of American foreign economic policy in the international trade field so far. The other principle is that of regional or political discrimination, which many people believe is desirable for its own sake and which is allowed under the rules of GATT (in the form of free trade areas and customs unions) so long as it meets rules of near-universality with respect to trade among the participants designed to ensure that the broad effect is to increase global freedom of trade. This exception to the GATT rules was never intended to sanction any arrangement so severely discriminatory as the European Economic Community, but was allowed to do so as a result of the American political interest in European economic and political integration. It was only as the United States became aware of the trade implications of the EEC that it was motivated to seek to mitigate the damage through the institution of the Kennedy Round of GATT negotiations.

Accession of Britain to membership of the Common Market would constitute another major step towards the institutionalisation of regional discrimination as the basic pattern of international trade, in contravention of the general post-war trend towards non-discriminatory reduction of barriers to international trade generally. In this context, the important change would be, not discrimination in trade in industrial goods, since tariff barriers on these are relatively low except for a rather small range of labour-intensive low-technology goods in which the developing countries have a comparative advantage over the developed countries that is frustrated by quotas as well as tariffs, but the adoption by Britain of the EEC's Common Agricultural Policy.

Trade in temperate-region agricultural products—cereals, and the products of livestock that feed on them—constitutes the great exception to the general trend towards more liberal international trade since the Second World War. All industrial countries place substantial barriers in the way of such trade, as an adjunct to domestic policies of relieving rural poverty through the support of prices paid to domestic farmers. That policy itself is a poor substitute for the economically efficient policy of accelerating the movement of rural workers off the land into industrial and service activities. The result of following it is to create a sharp conflict of interest between surplus producers such as the United States, Canada and Australia, interested in disposing of their surpluses in the world market, and importing countries such as Britain and, until recently, the EEC, which can find domestic markets for uneconomic domestic production at the expense of foreign producers of imports. This conflict is exacerbated by technical progress in agricultural production, and will become even more acute in future as a result of the "green revolution" in the developing countries, which promises to turn them from grain-deficit to grain-surplus countries.

Acceptance by Britain of the EEC's Common Agricultural Policy, on anything like present lines, would aggravate enormously the already serious problem of trade in temperate-zone agricultural products—apart entirely from the extra costs it would impose on the British economy. The British market would be pre-empted for the support of Continental farmers, and violently closed or virtually closed to the food-surplus countries; in the course of time, Europe would emerge as yet another surplus country attempting to press unwanted surplus grain on a reluctant world market.

This prospect is a matter of most serious concern for the American Government; and its consequences could be disastrous for the entire future of international trading relationships. The Americans, beleaguered by the combination of an overvalued currency and the resulting import competition, the concentration of import competition on politically-sensitive labour-intensive and regionally-concentrated industries, and growing official trade union protests against the "export of American jobs" implicit in direct foreign investment by the large U.S. corporations, have rapidly been retreating into a protectionist and isolationist mood. The Nixon Administration has been compelled to fight a rearguard action in favour of the existing degree of freedom in international trade and against the mounting tide of protectionist demands. Britain's acceptance of an agricultural policy that explicitly benefited European farmers at the expense of American agricultural exports might prove to be the last straw. The United States might well give way to internal protectionist pressures, and in the course of doing so espouse a regionalist approach to international trading relationships that would have the effect of pinning Britain even more firmly into a European dependent status rather than a world-wide trading role.

This possibility is particularly serious because there are signs that public opinion in the United States is paying increasing attention to the one alternative to protectionism and regionalism that seems viable at the present time—formation of a free trade association among like-minded countries. The GATT approach to the freeing of international trade, with its emphasis on non-discrimination in tariff reductions, seems to have reached a dead end. Of the two aspects of the traditional basis of contemporary American foreign trade policy—non-discrimination, and reciprocity—reciprocity has been increasingly emphasised, and non-discrimination less and less extolled as a fundamental moral principle in trade negotiations. A proposal for a free trade association involving Britain, the U.S.A. and other countries might capture the essence of this changing mood, and permit a further movement towards global trade liberalisation within the confines of the GATT rules to substitute for a retreat into protectionism and regionalism.

British accession to the Common Market will in all probability mean a halt to the progressive liberalisation of international trade that has characterised the post-war period, and a blockage of the only avenue by which the United States might be induced to abandon its current retreat into protectionism.

In assessing the probable shape of future events, it is also important to take account of the position and possible influence of Japan. As a defeated and initially underdeveloped country which the Americans have been anxious to build up as an ally against Communist China, Japan has enjoyed a specially favoured position in world trading relationships as regards her commercial, agricultural and foreign internal investment policies—though on the export side she has suffered from persistent discrimination against her manufacturers. But the logic of her economic structure and geographical location gives her increasingly a strong interest in freedom of trade and investment in the Pacific region. A scheme for a Pacific Free Trade Association, with special provisions favouring the exports of the Pacific developing countries, has been promoted with increasing appeal in the region over the past five years or so. If the United States became sufficiently dissatisfied with the terms on which Britain gained access to the EEC, the result might be, not merely a negative retreat into protectionism on the part of the United States, but a positive willingness to consider a regional trading arrangement based on the Pacific, in place of the basically trans-atlantic though nominally non-discriminatory arrangements that have dominated international trade policy-making so far.

The possible effects of British entry into the EEC in accentuating current tendencies towards American protectionism and the regionalisation of world trade are only one aspect—though probably the most important aspect—of the implications of British entry for the structure of the world economy. Another aspect which may prove to be of great significance is the plan for a common European currency, to which Britain is already committed if she joins. This plan is both ambiguous in the extreme in its origins, and problematical in its outcome. It combines two separate and contradictory motivations. The first is that the retreat from the Common Agricultural Policy necessitated by the devaluation of the franc and revaluation of the mark in 1969 must be atoned for, and the momentum of progress towards an integrated economic community be maintained, by commitment of the members of the EEC to the establishment of a common currency and the consequential harmonisation of policies that would make a repetition of 1969 impossible. The second is that if Europe did have a common currency and a single overall monetary policy, that currency could become a rival to the United States dollar as a world currency, and the central monetary policy could be used to combat the transmission of inflation from the United States to Europe, through an appropriate revaluation against the dollar. The establishment of a common European currency, which would in all probability be dominated by the City of London, is clearly an attractive proposition for Britain, at least superficially.

The problem is that the establishment of a common currency will entail the sacrifice to a central authority of a vital element in national sovereignty as currently conceived—the right to use monetary policy to pursue the national goals of full employment, price stability, and growth, together with the right to rectify errors if need be by a change in the exchange value of the national currency. Moreover, the need to make this sacrifice can be postponed indefinitely by the slow adoption of superficially important but in fact trivial transitional steps, such as narrowing the range of exchange variation among the community currencies and arranging for formal consultation on and co-ordination of national fiscal and monetary policies. The likelihood is that the pursuit of a common currency, in the absence of underlying agreement to sacrifice national sovereignty to the necessary extent, will simply paralyse the structure of European exchange rates, expose Europe even more irretrievably than heretofore to the pressures of American-initiated inflation, and contribute to the growth of the U.S. dollar as the world's international money. The City is already deeply committed—has had to become committed—to conducting its financial transactions in terms of U.S. dollars. The effort to develop a common European currency is more likely to put Europe *de facto* on the dollar standard than to produce a viable European currency capable of competing with the dollar.

In summary, British membership of the EEC is likely to contribute to a reversal of the post-war trend towards increasing integration of the world economy through trade liberalisation and increasing freedom of international capital movements. The results would be adverse both for the developing countries, whose development is already discriminated against by the trade policies of the developed countries, and for Britain herself, given her extended trading interests in the world outside Europe. The adoption of the commitment to a common European currency is especially dangerous for Britain, since on the one hand it will involve a binding commitment to a fixed exchange rate, which past experience has shown to be a serious impediment to the pursuit of domestic policy objectives, and on the other hand it will probably increase the dominance of the U.S. dollar and of American monetary policy in the world economy—quite contrary to the objectives of the "Europeans".

PART FOUR

The Alternatives

XI

THE STRATEGIC ISSUES

by Leonard Beaton

Former Director of Studies of the Institute of
Strategic Studies

THE GROWTH OF a serious movement for the political
union of Western Europe has put Britain into a profound
dilemma. Attempts to unify this great area have a long history;
and if there is one classic precept of British foreign policy it is
that Britain's independence can only be sustained if a united
Continent can be prevented. British troops and money were
consistently devoted to this objective over the centuries.

British government opposition to the growth of a union
through the Monnet mechanism—a customs union followed by an
economic union followed by a presumed need for political
authority followed by political union—was predictable and did
indeed come : but apart from the welcome nationalism of President de Gaulle it could find no *point d'appui*. It was consistently
blunted by several factors. First, the Monnet inversion of the
usual processes of politics left the whole question ambiguous.
While no one could doubt that Napoleon or Hitler was unifying
the Continent, a substantial sector of British opinion seriously
doubted whether Dr Hallstein could or would do it. Secondly,
British foreign policy had tied itself to the United States and had
been built on the premise that the only safe Europe was one
which enjoyed the full power of the United States in its daily life.
As it happened, the U.S. was fascinated with the prospect of a
European union which it believed would solve the European
security problem, release American power and contain what
dangerous elements may remain in European politics. Thirdly
(admittedly in the context of preliminary failure), a fundamental
if unconsidered change entered into official life. Officials and
then governments not only abandoned the traditional policy of

keeping the Continent divided to maintain British independence, but became convinced that there was no future for Britain outside European union. The assumption that the central objective of British policy was to preserve the nation's independence and institutions was reversed.

In economic policy, the sudden discovery that a new economic principle—the large home market—has become central to all industry and commerce[1] at least provided a coherent proposition around which debate and thought could gather. but the political considerations, which have probably been the decisive ones, are so riddled with contradictions as to be almost impossible to discuss.

The fundamental difficulty is quite simply this. Such men as Mr Edward Heath, Mr Harold Wilson and Lord Gladwyn are quite aware of the varieties of national state with their governments, their systems of justice, their armed forces, their foreign policies. They have made it clear that they do not believe that this is what is being formed in Europe. Equally, they are well aware of the alliance relationship, a technique on which British policy has always depended and does today more than ever before. It cannot be this which they expect to derive from what is called the political union of Europe, since a grand alliance already exists in NATO and since significant economic sacrifices are being urged on the country to allow it to join in the construction of this great new thing. What they are advocating is something they consider to be new : and it is therefore extremely difficult to assess what they are trying to do. They feel, or seem from their statements to feel, that it is possible for the British, French, Germans and others to enter into an arrangement which goes far deeper than NATO or any other existing association and yet which stops short of being a state. The words of the Prime Minister, Mr Heath, are quite clear on this point. First, the absence of any British intention to enter a political federation :[2]

"Those members of the Community who want a federal system, but who know the views of Her Majesty's Government and the Opposition parties here are prepared to forgo their

[1] This in spite of the much greater success of the continental European economies in the 1950s in contrast with the United States; and of Japan, Canada, Sweden and Australia in the 1960s in contrast with the United States and the Common Market.

[2] House of Commons debates, February 25th, 1970, col. 1221.

federal desires so that Britain should be a member and take part in political consultation and co-ordination with them."

Yet the assurance that this will be more than what now exists:[1]

> "Some hon. Members opposite, including the right hon. Member for Battersea, North (Mr Jay), believe that it is better that we as a country should go it alone and that we can exercise equal influence. Surely the last few years have shown that this is no longer the case. There are some who take this view, including some of my right hon. and hon. friends. They would argue that the lack of influence over the past few years has been due to particular Government policies. That may be a contributory factor, but does not comprise the whole of the factors about the influence of a single country in the modern world today. I respect their disagreement, but I believe that we have to play a part with others if it is possible to do so."

Had this statement been made in 1948, it would have been a piece of advocacy for the Western alliance. But read in the context of a thriving alliance structure, it is clear that when Mr Heath talks about going it alone he means the sort of situation that has prevailed in the last decade. Thus, the four-power confrontation with the Soviet Union over Berlin, the acquisition of American nuclear delivery systems, the permanent stationing of tens of thousands of men in Germany, and so on, constitute a situation which falls within the broad definition of going it alone. Thus a Europe which achieved what NATO has achieved—in which common commands held the assignment of common troops, in which nuclear planning was done by joint authorities, in which fleets were exercised in common, in which immense quantities of military equipment were exchanged, in which major projects (like the Harrier) were done jointly, and in which a deeply difficult military crisis was passed without any break in the ranks—would be one in which Mr Heath would define as Britain going it alone. He wants something different: "to play a part with others". On occasions, he has gone so far (with Lord Gladwyn, among others) as to talk about something entirely new in political life. The elements of this, it seems, are to be found in the methods of the EEC; the supreme authority will be an

[1] *Ibid.*, col. 1220.

agency (presumably a Council of Ministers) under the direct orders of Governments; the voting system, however conceived, will in practice not exercise authority over major states against their will.

It would be a proper conclusion from this orthodox British governmental and official position that the new Europe will not on this basis achieve anything which can be called political union. It is also reasonable to assume that since the Atlantic grouping has already achieved more than such a group can aspire to, and that with the U.S. as a member it is far more able to make its way in the world, any intimate inner group that is formed will have no significant function not already performed at the wider level. Two qualifications to this must, however, be made. The first is that many unionists who are allowing Mr Heath and Mr Wilson to speak for the European cause believe that there is no point in exposing the British public to the full consequences of their actions. Taking their cue and usually their ideas from American continental ideologists, they are convinced that a united Europe is manifest destiny. They are content that what they regard as a move into quicksands should be advertised as a gentle and hesitant first step holding out no obligations for later steps. In other words, this powerful school of opinion thinks it can see the grain of history and is convinced that the act of "joining Europe" (as they so curiously express it) will bring with it the consequences so vehemently denied by its authors. Many of this school of opinion believe that Mr Heath is one of them while Mr Wilson is not.

The second qualification is that there is a small but possibly influential group of people who see membership in the EEC as a useful political tactic. The argument is that either with or without an intimate American alliance (a matter which is mainly up to the Americans themselves) Britain must not allow it to be thought that she is outside the mainstream of European development. The European movement is a fact; and while it is most unlikely (on this view) to lead to a union, the French have stolen a distinct advantage on the British by being willing to make the unionist noises and join in grandiose proclamations. This makes it easier for them to achieve their objects of policy with other European states and would also make it easier for them to wield power in Washington if, like the British, they wanted to. This argument can be taken a stage further. It can be held that an intimate Anglo-French alliance of the post-Second World War type remains a primary national objective. This view is widely represented among influential Tories. Alternatively, it can be argued that Joseph Chamberlain's priorities were right; that the logical British policy should be based on the Americans and the West Germans rather than the European particularism of the French; and that the twin pillars of such a policy are NATO and the Common Market (in which the pro-American policies and primarily industrial economies of the British and Germans will predominate). This last is the only school of opinion in favour of joining which exhibits any degree of sophistication. The European policy of the 1964-70 Labour Governments suggests that it was pursuing a Washington-London-Bonn axis and that it was persuaded that membership in the EEC would contribute to this by allowing Britain to speak in the name of Europe in Washington and by undermining the Bonn-Paris axis.

Amid these remarkable contradictions of outlook and objective, an assessment of the strategic implications of British membership in the EEC is exceptionally difficult. Those who are to dispute the effects must first agree on the likely consequences : union or no union; government or no government; NATO surviving effectively or a breach with the Americans; an Anglo-French Europe, an Anglo-German Europe or a real tripartite operation; or just another meaningless Western European Union. Both sides of the debate tend to cling to one class of these assumptions for their favourable effects and then abandon them when confronted with unfavourable effects. The tendency to do this at the official and political level has reached the proportions of a scandal.

Membership in the EEC carries with it no significant political commitments, apart from the customs union, the Agricultural Policy and the common commercial policy.[1] It therefore has no strategic implications of consequence. This is obvious if one observes its effect on France, West Germany or any of the others.

What one must consider, therefore, is the probable effect of a

[1] As the original EEC was, in effect, the unification of the existing trade and commercial structure of the six countries (involving, for example, no loss of free entry for any existing supplier), the political effects were small. The same would not be true of British entry since this has been negotiated not on the principles of the Rome Treaty but on the words of it; and these words were not drawn up to include Britain. Thus, a drastic alteration in world trade is involved and the political effects of this are important.

British European policy which continues in the direction imparted to it by the European consciousness of Mr Wilson and Mr Heath. A great range of questions is opened up by this. One might consider the possible relations of a unified Europe with a Soviet Union which continues to rule many discontented Eastern Europeans; the effect on the Soviet-American relationship of the emergence of a power which was richer and more vigorous than either (though gravely deficient in natural resources); the means by which a European great power would define and enforce its strategic interest in the Mediterranean, the Middle East and Africa; the kind of settlement that four Continental powers (Europe, the Soviet Union, America, China) might seek and the hegemony that they might exercise, singly or jointly, over the remaining small powers; the other unions which so loud a proclamation of the need to be continental would provoke; and the shape which these powers might try to give their nuclear forces in order to survive in such a world. Here, however, I propose to look at only three questions which must be at the forefront of debate : the fate of the Atlantic alliance, the impact on the specifically British contribution to security, and the significance of European political unity for the building of a world order.

Whether organically unified or not, a European political union will seek to form a powerful unit within the Atlantic alliance. The United States State Department has long dreamed of a second pillar to the alliance which they see as in some way equivalent to the United States. This image is in large measure imaginary. Apart from the Marshall Plan romantics who see themselves as the fathers of a great new America, the serious policymakers in Washington divide into those who see European union as a way of escaping finally from the NATO tangle and those who do not believe a union can happen. The first of these schools of opinion represents a serious threat to British and European strategic interests. It is exceptionally difficult to see how any sustained defence of western Europe could be maintained even if there was a central government able to organise the resources of the area : the problem is more difficult still with ten Governments, ineffective institutions, no power to tax or conscript, and no acknowledged centre of decisions over war and peace.

At the level of internal alliance bargaining, there is a real difficulty about the two-pillar concept. This is that it is hard to negotiate from a position which is itself a difficult compromise. Curiously in view of the implications of his own policy,[1] this point has been noticed by Mr Heath, though in answer to the argument that Britain and the Six could work together in W.E.U. :[2]

> "There is no doubt that when the Community starts working seriously together in political and military matters, then the W.E.U. will lose its usefulness as a forum in which we can take part. This is for the simple reason that, having thrashed out economically[2] defence problems among themselves, the Six will not then want to go to the W.E.U. and thrash the matter out all over again with us as an outside member."

The future American relationship with European security is clearly one of the ambiguities in the European debate. A latent resentment of American predominance in alliance affairs has shown itself among many Europeanists, both in Britain and in France. What might be called the Suez Syndrome is still strong, especially among Conservatives, and the discovery of Europe by Mr George Brown (as he then was) brought with it an indignant rejection of the "junior partnership" which Churchill had so carefully constructed as a means of introducing American power into Europe. There is, however, another and more serious line of argument. This is that the Americans may be leaving Europe; and that if they are there must be a European security structure able to accept the load.

On the substantive danger of renewed American isolationism, Britain must decide first whether she likes junior partnership (in the manner of Sir Alec Douglas-Home) or dislikes it (in the manner of Lord George-Brown). If, as she should, she likes it, the problem is how to sustain it. While the Americans say they would like a united Europe, in fact they will not like the consequences. When they find it hard to work with, they will detach themselves. The hold of the British on the sympathies of the Americans is unique now as it was in 1940. A close American involvement with Britain is a central element in their continuing commitment to Europe. Such a relationship means being a junior partner and it means acting in such a way as to sustain the American

---

[1] House of Commons Debates, February 25th, 1970, col. 1221.

[2] This is as recorded in *Hansard*. Presumably the words used were "economic and..."

belief that this is a real and enduring unity. It is on this belief
that, for example, the irreversible sharing of American nuclear
secrets with Britain took place. A united Europe will inevitably
be seen by the U.S. as a power which could become a rival. As
Europe presumed to claim equal control, especially in a crisis, the
American fear of being committed to a conflict they could not
manage would grow. If anything in politics can be predicted, it is
that an alliance of two giants will drift apart, as the Sino-Soviet
alliance did. Those who seek such a solution to Europe's dependence on American power are consistent, though over-optimistic
about their own safety; those who pretend that they are merely
insuring against American isolationism seem unaware of the part
they are playing in fulfilling their prophecy. Both classes, however, lack seriousness because neither shows the slightest sign that
they recognise the implications in terms of central authority, men
or weapons of a Western Europe responsible for its own security.

Britain has played a major part in world security over a period
of centuries; in our own time the strategic importance of the
British position in the Middle East, the Persian Gulf, South-East
Asia, the Indian Ocean and (to a lesser extent) in Africa has been
very great. These commitments are changing with decolonisation,
Soviet penetration and the development of a new, if ill-defined,
system of power in the post-colonial world. The shape which
British bases and British undertakings would take in the absence
of any European evolution would depend on the decisions of the
government of the day. It seems clear, however, that the conviction of many Commonwealth Governments (and of others like
Jordan or the Persian Gulf sheikhdoms with an old relationship
with Britain) that Britain is the only major power they trust
would not have changed. Whether British governments choose to
build on this, and whether the reputation for helping friends in
trouble is worth the cost, is a large question of judgment. My
own view is that the resources expended and priorities chosen
over the 1950-70 period were on the whole justified. The only
objection which might be made is that British Governments
preferred (as they did with the Empire) to leave others ignorant
of what they were doing. As the American conviction took hold
that they alone carried the burdens of security, what Britain
self-evidently required was not abdication or European chauvinism but public relations campaigns about the nature of the real
world.

There is no natural logic by which British membership in the EEC or some political union should lead to the abandonment of Britain's world-wide relationships. In political terms, however, it has had this effect.[1] The European period has coincided with the growth of general Western disillusion with commitments to the small and weak, a mood which was greatly reinforced by the need to produce a critique of the Vietnam affair. As the 1960s progressed, it became conventional for Americans and others to ask what they were doing in so distant a Continent as Asia—a question which did not occur in the Japanese or Korean wars. British opinion reflected this; and the imperial emotions which had affected conservative and official opinion simultaneously faded away with the antics of post-colonial Commonwealth politicians. So did the sentimental Labour belief in a multi-racial association for its own sake. In this context, the primitive notion of a new European destiny gave the excuse needed to abandon responsibilities which served the West as a whole without credit and which carried with them enormous potential liabilities.

Membership in the EEC itself would terminate most of the commercial relationships which were the original source of most of Britain's world-wide political relationships. Success in unifying the foreign policy of a European group would mean that foreign countries would no longer be dealing with Britain but would be dealing with a great new power. Such a power could not expect to inherit the benign (if complex) relations of Britain and her former colonies. Put more simply, the specific British contribution to world security would be transformed on being absorbed into a European policy. Most of the political relationships on which it is based would disappear. This would relieve the country of certain burdens[2] and deprive the world order of a part of its cement. As with the transfer of Britain's world-wide commercial position to Japan and the United States, it must be recognised that much of the damage has already been done by a decade of determined

[1] Mr Edward Heath has been an interesting exception to the general rule that European unionists are also European isolationists. With their Continental liberal intellectual origins, most unionists have tended to ignore the realities of power both in the organisation of the state and in its international behaviour.

[2] British opinion has shown few signs of recognising the heavy new burdens likely to come with the formation of a European political union. If it comes to matching Soviet power in Europe without the Americans, the commitment will be heavy and enduring.

re-orientation towards a unified Europe, real or imagined.

The central strategic question of our time is the capacity of a dominant group of powers to do at least the minimum of what has to be done to ensure survival—in the safe organisation of nuclear weapons, in resisting the development of chemical, biological and environmental weapons, in stopping or controlling the spread of nuclear materials around the world, in handling high-level or low-level crises securely. Most of the great questions in the last quarter century have been resolved by a group led by the United States and Britain and given a grudging minimum of co-operation and assent by the Soviet Union. It is possible to argue that American-Soviet relations are improving to the point where the Soviet Union will take a full part in the world order. Whether or not this is so, the power of the Americans, and so of the order itself, depends critically on the group of substantial middle powers which are all aligned to a greater or lesser extent with the West. The four most important of these are Britain, France, West Germany and Japan—the first two with membership in the Big Four and the second two still limited by the tradition of defeat.

If three of these four join in a new political construction, they may or may not make it easier ultimately to build a working order. But it is likely that, as with China, the sense of change and development will make it impossible to make real progress for many years. Such a Europe will be absorbed in its internal life and anxious to exploit the full potential of its power before agreeing to any institutions which formalise the power structure. More than that, however, it would add one more giant to be absorbed. Medium and small powers work to find a place in the order of things because they do not have illusions of self-sufficiency. The giants go it alone, often to disaster. That is why a flexible, intelligent, alliance-minded Britain has so consistently survived and brought far mightier rivals to their knees. Britain was the main influence in fashioning the Concert of Europe; one of the main supports of the League of Nations; and a decisive influence in the growth of the present successful order based on the narrower circle of the Western alliance and the broader one of the U.N. As the northern province of a new European union, the particular energies of this particular people would be redirected to the self-sufficient ambitions of a continental power. The world order as we know it now would lose a valuable friend.

XII

FREE WORLD AND THE POLITICS OF
FREE TRADE

by Lionel Gelber

*Historian, author; formerly Special Assistant to
the Prime Minister of Canada.*

B R I T A I N H A S L O N G had one foot planted in Europe and another stretched across the seas. Her entry into the Common Market would alter that classic posture and, as she commits herself to narrow Eurocentric confines, recast adversely the power structure of the West. This is a danger that Washington itself has done much to promote. A more positive outcome is, nevertheless, still within reach. Even the latest phase in the struggle between free trade and protectionist elements in the United States will not have been futile if it prompts Americans to think again. It should, moreover, remind everyone of the degree to which politics and economics interact not only at home but on the world scene. For new economic measures may be conceived that, from a politico-strategic angle, might perpetuate a status for Britain consonant with her past and leave American primacy comparatively intact.

It will be hard, though, to get things done until there is more consistency on both sides of the Atlantic in achieving common purposes. Before the era of American primacy the British were masters in preconcerting co-operative steps with others all the world over. Even now, Anglo-American defence facilities are to be built at Diego Garcias, a British island in the Indian Ocean. Then, too, for the security of South East Asia and so as to sustain her presence East of Suez, Britain has just concluded a consultative pact with four overseas members of the Commonwealth—Australia, New Zealand, Malaysia and Singapore. But while she was negotiating this agreement, she was also negotiating with the Six over the terms upon which they would let her enter the European Economic Community. Eventually moves like these could be at odds—such is the confusion attending the great debate over whether Britain should join, and thereby enlarge, the EEC. The more the British are Europeanised the less may be the latitude they retain for banding together, as they please, with others.

If Western Europe does more for its own defence the West is strengthened, and towards this objective a Euro-group within the North Atlantic Alliance has been formed. The Common Market may take credit for completing the job which NATO encouraged—one, namely, of substituting a wary partnership between France and West Germany for what, in Western Europe, has been the most devastating of feuds. To clinch that *rapprochement,* however, an enlargement of the European Community was not required. Nor is it required even though a grim recent increase in Soviet preparedness has compelled NATO Europe to shoulder what, under the Nixon Doctrine, is Western Europe's own bigger proportion of the load. President Nixon could thus keep more American troops in Western Europe for the interim than most of the Senate has wished. Doubts in Western Europe about the use of the American deterrent on Europe's behalf could also be shelved momentarily. But throughout (as Washington should now appreciate) there has been no evidence that membership by Britain in the European Community would improve the performance of that entity in the field of defence. Omens of another sort can be discerned. "Ah Madam", was Bernard Shaw's presumed retort to Isadora Duncan, "What if our child has my body and your brains?" If Britain joined the European Community she could implement her view of world order only if most of the other major components shared it with her. Their view of world order may not be the same. It might be the one that prevails.

What Britain needs, what the West needs for Britain, is an alternative to outright Europeanisation. This she could find through a treaty for multilateral free trade between Western industrial countries outside the EEC. So wide-ranging a pact might also cover non-tariff barriers together with temperate-zone agriculture. Such a venture may be undertaken in accordance with article 24 of GATT (the General Agreement on Tariffs and Trade). It could extend from the European Free Trade Association in Western Europe to North America and across the Pacific to the Antipodes, perhaps even up to Japan. If the United States sponsors a world-wide project of that kind, it may serve, on politico-strategic as well as economic grounds, crucial interests of her own. Crucial British interests might also be served. Through a multilateral free trade treaty Britain could obtain access to markets as big as the Common Market without having to pay the heavy toll, financial and political, which Europeanisation would extort in other respects.

The United States is the mainstay of the West and the West will suffer from anything which augments trends inimical to the American role. In the Common Market these have been curbed until now. Upon its enlargement, however, they could get out of hand. The West is not only conjuring with the admission of Britain and other applicants to the European Community; if they enter the rest of non-Soviet Europe will rush to join. Not that all further applicants would be admitted without demur. Spain and even Portugal (despite her EFTA membership) may first have to change regimes; neutrals, lest they be arrayed with one camp against the other, must take care. But the West will be set back if, through a heedless redistribution of power, it becomes politically and strategically unstable. As long as the EEC remains moderate in size, less harm may be wrought by any self-regarding, inward-looking tendencies. But once enlarged, its faults would be writ large. Six rather than Ten could well be its optimum.

If Britain stays out, the EEC would lack further major recruits. Still valid, as it will be argued later on, should be the case for a multilateral free trade area. Meanwhile, from the perspective of Western unity, it is essential to recall divisive issues which the French have raised and which, in another guise, the West Germans, wittingly or unwittingly, could be the next to aggravate. When General de Gaulle twice vetoed British entry into the Common Market, one salient motive was his objection to that Anglo-American friendship which had saved France and to ties which had persisted between Britain and other countries of the Commonwealth. These residual boons, vestiges of an oceanic legacy, might, in a favourable atmosphere, be highly prized. The atmosphere was unfavourable, however, when Britain was being groomed for a continental berth. It may therefore have been no accident if a Prime Minister as Eurocentric in outlook as Mr Edward Heath attempted at the White House and on a national American network to downgrade semantically the special relationship with the United States while, at the same time, provok-

ing the most gratuitous of Commonwealth crises over the sale of
naval arms to South Africa. In France, and elsewhere, Gaullist
sentiment did not expire with the General. And in spite of
Britain's willingness to appease a lingering Gaullist viewpoint the
terms laid down at Brussels might still be stiff. Yet signals flashed
by Mr Heath, tacit but fraught with compliance, could not go
unnoticed across the Channel.[1]

Britain's entry bid has been a spectacle dogged by paradox.
Rather than lock out the British from the charmed circle, the
French have always had the most puissant of reasons for inducing
them to join. Upon entering the European Community, the
Elsyée Palace may presuppose more than ever, Britain might

[1] Since the 1962-63 negotiations many of the most influential of
British opinion media have been trying to prepare Britain for Europeanisation by playing down historic overseas ties. In 1961-62, for example, the
BBC ran two talks, reprinted in *The Listener,* depicting Anglo-American
friendship as an unhistorical myth. The writer referred to this in *Foreign
Affairs*, New York, January 1963, p. 321 and added that truth is a myth
for those who have myths of their own to purvey.

Not only Anglo-American friendship but also broad issues such as
Commonwealth bonds were treated to one-sided manipulation with a bias
that was tacit and subtle, intrusive and prolonged. See Lionel Gelber,
The Alliance of Necessity (Stein and Day, New York, 1966; Robert Hale
Ltd., London, 1967) pp. 54-60; 62-67.

The major American opinion media merely relayed across the Atlantic
the Europeanising efforts of their British counterparts—those, too, of
Westminster and Whitehall. Thus Washington, with Ottawa, may have a
lot to do if an impasse occurs at Brussels, or if Parliament, reflecting the
will of the British people, rejects the final terms. See Lionel Gelber in *The
New Statesman*, London, December 18th, 1970, pp. 825-826.

In an article in *The Spectator,* London, January 9th, 1971, pp. 45-46,
the writer suggested that Mr Heath, on his first trip to Ottawa and
Washington as Prime Minister, was striving to mobilise American and
Canadian opinion on behalf of Europeanising policies which, as British
opinion polls have overwhelmingly shown, the bulk of his own compatriots
repudiated.

Perhaps a shorter Common Market campaign could have swept the
British people off their feet. Even now, there are few adequate outlets on
either side of the Atlantic at the disposal of those who have sought to warn
against the Europeanisation of Britain. As a result most of the British
people have recoiled of their own accord—a sign of a political maturity
which the West might well lose if Britain is swallowed up by a European
union.

On how opinion media demand free expression for themselves but
withhold it from others, see Lionel Gelber, *The American Anarchy*, New
York, 1953, pp. 140-175.

collaborate with France as an offset to the economic preponderance of the West Germans, to their ensuing political superiority as well. But if, in this context, the French have now outsmarted themselves, few beyond the Six will weep.

Junior members of the Common Market deserve more sympathy. It has been their conviction that, with Britain as a member, they would gain a champion not only against the West Germans but also against the French. Current realities are less Eurocentric. It no longer matters to other, more numerous non-members, whether, in the EEC, the West Germans or the French exert most influence. There is only the western section of the pre-war Reich, as *Ostpolitik* has again underscored, to consider. Western Europe itself, moreover, is now merely a key sector in a global balance by which the European balance of power has been supplanted. The game is being played with bigger counters and the question is whether Western Europe should become one of these. It is not whether the French or West Germans will vie with each other within the EEC, but for what, beyond the EEC, an enlarged Community may be tempted to combine.

The French, after all, should have recovered by now from the trauma of World War II. They do not seem to have done so. Though the French Navy and Air Force again participate in some joint exercises with their Western allies, France still hampers those who have underwritten her defence by having NATO evicted from French territory; by crass zig-zags in the Middle East which, for the sake of Arab oil and her own Afro-Asian ambitions, have been more pro-Russian than pro-Western in effect. Nor has France expressed regret for trying to disrupt the national unity of Canada, an ally that went to her rescue in two world wars. A local domination by the Bonn Republic may worry its neighbours and injure French pride. France might fall back on a neo-colonial "Francophonie" (one that spreads from French-speaking Africa to French-speaking Quebec) with which to console herself culturally, economically and even as a merchandiser of arms. This would be a diversion from the Rhine not without a French nineteenth-century precedent. But France is no longer to the fore as a bulwark of the West. Britain, on the other hand, might continue as one—if, that is, Franco-German tension within the European Community does not involve her and she eludes the ambivalence which that entity, torn between the parochially Eurocentric and its broader allegiance to the West, can generate.

The tangibles and intangibles of Britain's scattered oceanic legacy may have shrunk. What is left tallies, nevertheless, with the global dimensions of world politics in the new age. It also remains Britain's principal source of strength. That is why she cannot be deprived of it and still carry the same weight among European neighbours with their own Continental sources of strength. Yet, curiously enough, it was de Gaulle's constitutional intransigence which, if Britain had joined the Common Market, could have delayed her loss of overseas ties—or even deferred the risk which the enlarged EEC might pose to the comity of the West. Under President Pompidou the French have been contemplating a confederal apparatus within the European Community through which, stage by stage, economic and monetary union could be elaborated. The Treaty of Rome is slanted towards a pooling of sovereignty. Against a total pooling, if the Common Market is not to stagnate or collapse, Paris cannot hold out indefinitely.

Time after time in the twentieth century American power has preserved the West from defeat. Only through political as well as economic unification could the United States, despite all that is so defective in her federal system, exploit her own cumulative potential to the utmost. If the EEC is to do the same, it must within its more restricted fold, take a leaf from the American book. Membership for Britain in the EEC would thus differ in kind rather than degree from membership in other international bodies. Its grip on her life, as on the life of every component, would be at once more thoroughgoing and more unremittingly cohesive. If the European Community is to act like a single state it will have to endow itself with the ramified attributes of statehood. And it is as a single state that, as it evolves, it must act more and more.

Much that is centrifugal in the Common Market staves off the pull of the federalising, the supranational, the organic. Obstacles of language, race, traditions and living standards were not so steep when Bismarck, crushing the Hapsburgs and the French to create the German Empire, made the most of the *Zollverein*. But until the European Community acquires an authentic organic character it cannot attain its own aims. And if it does acquire an organic character an overriding sovereignty will emerge which, in the nature of things, forbids each member State of the Union from retaining separate exterior bonds. This aspect of a federal constitution is one with which Americans, Canadians and Australians are perfectly familiar. As a component of a European union, in other words, Britain must abandon a Commonwealth which, with surviving imponderables, still revolves around her and which, with trade preferences that are still so advantageous, it would be improvident to squander. London will not be able to speak at Washington or elsewhere for itself, and only Brussels, if that is to be the capital of the enlarged Community, can be heard.

What must tell is not a rigid, abstract preconception but administrative exigencies. It has long been foreseen that there would have to be a single currency, the harmonisation of laws between national units in the domains of taxation, welfare and employment if, as a single entity, so compact a complex as the Common Market is to function as well as it can.[1] A federalising process will thus have been started and nothing may do more than Britain's entry to revive it or speed it up. A political union might still be paralysed by innate sectional discrepancies. Yet its mere enlargement would erect the framework for a Third Force, a vehicle for neutralist impulses and one by which American leadership might even be undercut.

Washington has deemed such aberrations improbable. For its own defence, after all, Western Europe depends on American guarantees, nuclear and conventional. But in a global balance the fate of the West European sector could still be decisive. The United States thus also depends on it. A European Community may get away with much when it knows it cannot be left in the lurch. Enlargement and unification could make it less circumspect and not more.

Such a free-wheeling aggregation was a goal towards which Charles de Gaulle aspired. And events have demonstrated that he was right to debar Britain from the Common Market if a loose

[1] On the problem of the pound sterling and the sterling area, see Lionel Gelber, *The Alliance of Necessity*, p. 86. For comment on "America and Americanisation", please see *ibid.*, pp. 31-34. That comment was borrowed from an article by the writer in *Foreign Affairs,* New York, January 1963, pp. 316-318.

Also "World Politics and Trade Strategy" by Lionel Gelber in *New Trade Strategy for the World Economy* (ed. by H. G. Johnson) London, Toronto, Buffalo, 1969, pp. 85-87, 88-90.

union came first with him, wrong if it was a Third Force. A Third Force, at any rate, could be the upshot of what, with colleagues from across the Atlantic, Europeanisers among the British have been seeking. British and Continental firms, it is contended, will have to merge if they are to escape from the clutches of American multi-national corporations; just as these titans of industry and technology must raze national boundaries for both production and sales, it is further averred, so must the governments on which, in the fields of contracts and research, they rely to a considerable extent. But against an analysis as sweeping as that two points may be made. For one thing Swiss multi-national firms contrive to prosper without a broad political foundation. Nor, secondly, is economic competition of the future sure to be conducted from bastions in a single neighbourhood, even if this expands. It is a more criss-cross pattern which multi-national corporations themselves may actually be weaving. There are giant firms that span the oceans as well as the English Channel and these have been branching out, wherever the political environment is congenial, in a number of directions. That may not be as easy for Britain to do if she is unduly concentrated upon the Eurocentric.

Multi-national corporations with an American home base have long permeated European economies. The American economy is what their trans-atlantic counterparts must want to permeate. Yet that is a many-sided vocation in which multi-national firms which are Anglo-European by origin have been faring well without Britain having to devalue her own status in world affairs. In developed countries, moreover, workers may call for higher, not lower, tariffs when industries circumvent domestic wage levels by going elsewhere. Rules have yet to be devised for enterprises with foci that are so far-flung.

What Britain must avoid is a step in which her last state would be worse than her first. Much has been said about a tug between the unfettered sovereignty of Parliament and renunciations of an irrevocable character to the European Community. But more than that would distinguish a British signature on the Treaty of Rome from one on the Charter of the United Nations or on the text of the North Atlantic Alliance. As a national unit, Britain, on being fully Europeanised, will have to drop out of such international bodies. Only the EEC could enrol and only through it would the British people be in contact with them. Nationalism when distorted has been a Moloch in the worship of which millions and millions have died. But that is not what entry into the Common Market is all about. Here, at rock-bottom, the contrast should be between a more intensive brand of sovereignty that may be set up across the Channel and a traditional one that would permit Britain still to co-operate extensively with others. Continental participants, with roots in land-power, will not have kicked away the irretrievable props of their economy and society if the European Community should ever dissolve. This precisely is what, after being Europeanised, Britain, long pivot of an oceanic system, may have done.

The City of London, with its exceptional function in world business and international finance, is a product of that system. But the City's function may decline and pass to some continental centre when Britain is Europeanised. Even if her oceanic system has diminished, Britain is still a clearing-house for the political transactions of the Commonwealth as well as for many financial ones beyond it. Other countries with more wealth and resources do not have so exceptional a function to discharge. Nor are these the only exceptional functions that have accrued. Exceptional, too, despite gross disparities in economic and political power, is Britain's special relationship with the United States. What, upon Europeanisation, will she receive in exchange for a role globally so unique? It will not enhance but impair her status.[1]

This, moreover, is a feature of Europeanisation that as a federal union the United States should have understood. But her own continental schooling, despite oceanic burdens taken over from the British, is what has shaped her attitude towards the problem of Britain and the EEC. With smaller associates who fear the French and West Germans, the British were expected by Washington to stick up for the rule of law, for the liberalisation of trade and, in the realm of defence, for keeping Western Europe on the right track. But if Britain turns away from the outer world, if she thus abjures overseas sources of strength, her capacity and desire to do so may ebb. She is renowned as an exponent of representative democracy and she will abide by it

[1] See "Britain's Status and the City of London" in Lionel Gelber, *The Alliance of Necessity*, pp. 82-91. If there is a West European currency, Europeanisation will be a threat to the City, as it will be to the Commonwealth and Anglo-American friendship, which should be assessed from the standpoint of history as well as economics.

when there is a lapse from it within the European Community. Major components among the Six do not inspire the same confidence.

An institution such as the European Commission (with authority stemming from the Treaty of Rome) is, after all, scarcely a model of representative democracy as this is interpreted by the English-speaking peoples. True, as a representative democracy, the French may yet live down the vagaries of the past two centuries and for recent Nazi infamies the West Germans may be making amends. But the more intimate the links that Europeanisation entails the more awkward their outcome might be. In Italy, for instance, the Centre may succumb as Communists and neo-Fascists battle for supremacy while, if the extreme Left gains office, its neutralist foreign policy (with the neutralist Yugoslavs next door) can undermine NATO's Mediterranean flank. For the European Community to enmesh Britain in such a constitutional imbroglio would be serious; and, as indicated, an even graver politico-strategic phase could be superimposed. On this ground alone a smaller, not a larger, Community will be less of a gamble for Britain and the West.

Nor is it only constitutional instability with which London may have to cope if, after Britain has been Europeanised, the European Community is more tightly unified. The nuclear position, within the West itself, would be less stable. Nobody knows how the enlarged European entity will dispose of British and French nuclear weapons. Its national components can hardly merge without their arms establishments doing the same. The result should be an amalgamation of British and French nuclear weapons into a single European deterrent. Such a device might or might not violate the nuclear anti-proliferation treaty. But not even Russia is as likely to be averse if *Ostpolitik* (put over either by Herr Willy Brandt or by one of his successors) should fully materialise; for the nonce, at any rate, Bonn's endeavours have sufficed to subdue most routine Soviet charges of West German revanchism. And so the Bonn Republic, now or later, may buy off Muscovite clamours against a European deterrent in the management of which West Germany could have a hand.

France, though, might balk. Her nuclear weapons have been a French makeweight against the ascendancy of the Bonn Republic in Western Europe and she will cling to them as long as she can. Yield she must if the enlarged Community is to be unified but, with her Gaullist bent, she may still combat what has been, for most of the West, centralised nuclear control. Until now the British nuclear deterrent has been co-ordinated with the overall American deterrent while even the French, despite their withdrawal from NATO command, have had to use many of the same facilities. Yet in the West there will still be more than one finger on a nuclear trigger if a European deterrent disengages from the overall American deterrent. That is a complication which, until now, London and Washington have always soft-pedalled. With China making her début as a nuclear power, Americans and Russians must keep an eye fixed on her as well as on each other. As a member of the European Community, however, Britain may also be destined to an incessant controversy with the French over centralised and decentralised nuclear controls—one from which the United States could not stand aloof.

None of these problems can be swept under the rug. Washington feels, nevertheless, that if the European Community is enlarged it will, by doing more for itself and the common weal, ease the American task—that of adjusting prerequisites abroad to a gargantuan repair job at home. The United States, all the same, has been supporting the enlargement of the European Community while quarrelling with that entity over its trade policies. When therefore President Nixon delivered to Congress his second annual report on foreign affairs, he reconciled thesis and antithesis with a synthesis that was more Bismarckian than Hegelian : "Two strong powers in the West would add flexibility to Western diplomacy." But they may do quite the opposite. If two strong powers bicker, the West, with America in the van, could be self-immobilised—a cheerless prospect when rivals that are dictatorships can operate with so much more speed. The assumption of the United States is that Western Europe will be tranquil constitutionally and, as an equal, behave internationally with prudence. What she assumes may, in the light of events, be wishfully premature.

In a global balance, moreover, there cannot be the same prerogatives for two strong powers one of which, even if enlarged, must still depend on the other for nuclear guarantees and a costly American presence. The United States and the Soviet Union have been discussing the limitation of strategic arms and some enthusiasts even suggested that enlargement would entitle the EEC to a seat with them at the top table. It would not. Seats at the

top table are for those who have built deterrents as formidable as
the two which superpowers deploy. The EEC does not propose to
build one. The United States keeps her allies informed and
Western Europe can only wait until the hour is ripe for East and
West also to discuss the mutual reduction of tactical and conventional arms. About flaws in their record the American people
have not been reticent. But neither have these been in the same
category as the mass wars of twentieth century Europe, the
decivilising ideologies, the scant resistance to savage dictatorships.
Strange therefore is the idea, purveyed on both sides of the
Channel and on both sides of the Atlantic, that if Western
Europe should ever speak with a single voice no political utter-
ances will be as mature.

Even the *Ostpolitik* of the Bonn Republic, fulfilled or unful-
filled, might be a portent. In accepting the break-up of the
pre-war Reich, permanently or provisionally, it bowed to realities. Concomitants of *Ostpolitik* in other spheres could be exceed-
ingly ill-timed. It is particularly expedient for Russia to have the
status quo consolidated on the European frontiers of the Soviet
imperium when she has China to watch, has a new global
springboard in the Middle East to utilise and strives to outflank
and sunder the free world by sea. Russia with West Germany
must get the consent of the United States, Britain and France
before they can arrive at an accommodation over Berlin. But
Moscow has also had to elicit the consent of East Germany—the
one client State on the European outskirts of the Soviet imperium
which, when Poland seethes with tumult once more, may retard
ideological subversion from the West. There is, besides, a new
Five Year Plan to quell similar unrest among Russian workers.
Nor does the Kremlin, apart from the arms race, have to abate its
outward imperialist thrust when Community Europe is so eager
to help Russia, with a severe conflict in priorities, get off the
hook. For should *Ostpolitik* resume, it is to be consummated by
economic deals which surpass in magnitude anything the Italians
and French have undertaken with the Soviet Union hitherto.
Bonn, moreover, delved into these with Moscow before Russo-
American talks on strategic arms limitation could bear fruit and
when Russia's own pursuit of European hegemony was again
revealed by her insistence that a European security conference
precede rather than coincide with agreement over mutual troop
reductions or withdrawals.

Irony abounds. Dean Acheson, an American elder statesman to whom the Bonn Republic owes much, called upon Britain to join the Common Market so that there might be an Anglo-French brake on a "mad race to Moscow". But that is an assignment for which both France and Britain could disqualify themselves by the warmth with which they commended Herr Willy Brandt, the West German Chancellor, for his efforts. The latter acknowledged that with her global responsibilities the United States must study how a variety of issues may impinge on each other. The Bonn Republic, according to him, had no commensurate obligation. A concept, self-engrossed and Euro-centric, thus cropped up—one from which come the economic modalities of *Ostpolitik* and in which all major elements of the European Community have appeared glad to participate.

It was Charles de Gaulle who equated American power, from which his country derived security, with Soviet power which made France insecure. And such was the Third Force logic that drew him behind the Iron Curtain. When the General's disciple, M. Georges Pompidou, followed Herr Brandt to Moscow, the President of France may only have been competing with the West German Chancellor for the Kremlin's *beaux yeux*. But trends could have been started with a momentum of their own. And in those the British at once began to take part. Courting Bonn, as well as Paris, for entry into the Common Market, they, like the French, lavished bipartisan praise on Herr Willy Brandt's version of *Ostpolitik* before its full consequences, politico-strategic and economic, could be seen. Nor was British trade and industry going to be outdone at Moscow by Britain's own prospective partners in the EEC. Then the blow descended. British companies, in conjunction with Russian officials, had been chalking out massive projects for the development of vast Siberian mineral resources. These, however, the Soviet Union eliminated from its ninth Five-Year Plan. Russia suggested that they also be talked over with the French and Japanese. She does not feel ready for a big Siberian copper project. It was more surprising, even if business *is* business, that this was the sole British consideration.

Incongruous, at any rate, have been concurrent British man-oeuvres. London has done most to warn that, with a Soviet breakthrough from the Middle East to the Indian Ocean, the oceanic approaches to Western Europe might be rendered more vulnerable. Proclaiming that these will be safer if Britain furnishes

South Africa with naval arms, she has risked the disintegration of the Commonwealth—though this can also have been done to impress upon Paris and Brussels the manner in which the mentality of Westminster and Whitehall has been Europeanised. But be that as it may, few junctures could have been as unpropitious for negotiating a series of industrial projects from which even Russian naval ship-building might gather fresh impetus. Then too if, as endorsed, Britain ever builds containers for Eurasian use on the trans-Siberian railway, Russia herself would be still more self-contained economically and strategically. The more she can switch her commercial traffic from the Suez or Cape routes, the less it will be a target for the navies of the West. *Ostpolitik* may or may not be ratified. But it has been accompanied by symptoms of a fever with Eurocentric fluctuations that are bound to recur.

About this, all the same, there is a mystery. Russia sets store on the industrial and technological concomitants of *Ostpolitik*. She covets equipment and expertise as advanced as any possessed by the West. Nobody explains, though, how she will pay for it. Barter can never fill the bill. It would take a capitalist economy to make capital out of the stupendous economic programme broached, with *Ostpolitik,* for Russia. She has diamonds to sell and the Kremlin sits, of course, on its gold but, as this is a last line of defence, it may flinch from putting that hoard into productive use. Closer ties between the two halves of Europe is an objective of the EEC. It will do what it can, with promptings from Bonn, to forge links through Comecon, the East European economic grouping. More than once President Nixon has pleaded for a state of affairs in which there could be normal trade between Russia and the United States. Washington, nevertheless, is now left with one sombre fact to ponder. On a number of global fronts Russia is pushing against the West harder than ever. Throughout, as if they do business on another planet, top-level industries in West Germany, France, Italy and Britain have been poised to enhance the technological prowess of the West's chief rival.[1]

---

[1] Lionel Gelber, "Britain, Russia and the Open Seas", *The Spectator,* London, October 31st, 1970, pp. 508-11.

For additional features of Soviet naval expansion, see a sub-chapter by the writer "Open Societies and the Open Sea" in *New Trade Strategy for the World Economy* (ed. H. G. Johnson), pp. 127-46.

And what these vacillations signify as far as the British are concerned should be manifest. They are signs of how, as long as Britain is oriented towards the EEC, she will tend to drift away from Atlantic moorings rather than fasten them down more firmly. Only by a countervailing American initiative can that drift be circumscribed.

No drift from Atlantic moorings is calculated to break hearts in the Kremlin. At the outset Moscow suspected, with more realism than Washington or London, the degree to which a Third Force potential may reside in the enlargement and unification of the European Community. Normally a cluster of Powers with neutralist propensities could be as much of a nuisance at Moscow as at Washington and that, for the Kremlin, would not have been a welcome situation. But *Ostpolitik*, despite the fresh travail of the Czechs and Russian bad faith in the Middle East, has supervened. If a Third Force now emerged it would be one in which Bonn no longer fanned the embers of West German irredentism. And thus transmuted, it could further two sinister interrelated Soviet aims. In a Gaullist vein it may, first of all, loosen strands between Western Europe and the United States. Secondly, if the sequel to *Ostpolitik* is a growing dependence on joint economic schemes with Russia, the EEC might hesitate more and more to offend her on major European issues or to pit itself against her in other global theatres. While the West Europeans penetrate the Soviet imperium with their technology the Russians could respond with a penetration that politically and strategically tends to dislocate the West.

This might become a design for power, reminiscent of Rapallo and the Nazi-Soviet Pact, with the Soviet Union in Germany's place and with the European victims as unteachable as ever. In Herr Brandt's own vision of *Ostpolitik* there have been American and NATO underpinnings. But neither he nor his critics are immortal; though he may forge a two-edged sword he cannot forecast how it will be swung or by whom.[1] If there is no *Ostpolitik* to embolden her, Russia might decry the enlargement and unification of the European Community. But if *Ostpolitik* is

[1] One comparatively minor test might soon arise. With American backing Radio Free Europe, Munich, broadcasts news of the outer world behind the Iron Curtain. Moscow, however, might deem its activities incompatible with *Ostpolitik*. If so, will Washington, at Bonn's request, shut that station down?

carried out, the Soviet Union may even discover some less primitive method of financing its own technological progress. The unpredictability of the EEC as a Third Force could detract from the unity of the West when its unity is still so imperative. Less unpredictable would be a wider European sway for Russia herself.

And for the United States, with her stake in Western Europe as a rampart of the West, this might be one of the most disquieting of contingencies. When he submitted to the Congress his second general report on foreign affairs, President Nixon rebuked Moscow for attempts at European concord that were selective and self-serving. "A differentiated détente, limited to the USSR and certain Western allies but not others", said the President, "would be illusory." But here, surely, Russia can do little by herself. What should perplex the United States is the willingness of major powers in Western Europe to play along. On illusion, after all, the Kremlin has no monopoly. "A differentiated détente" could prefigure a Third Force and, though Americans have long pressed for the Europeanisation of Britain, less will go amiss if there is a smaller rather than a larger Community.

The true scale of things, contrariwise, may yet be exemplified by "ping pong diplomacy" between Washington and Peking. Bonn and her sympathisers earn praise; but they neglect to reckon with the interests of the West as a whole. So also, it will be a losing game not only for Britain herself if, intent upon Europeanisation, she pares down overseas ties. A Third Force would ignore the dimensions of the world contest and they are what *Ostpolitik* disregarded. Bonn went astray when it treated matters which should have been reserved for a broad global settlement as local or regional ones. And that was no trivial blunder. For the West thus had some of its best cards irretrievably thrown away when it has none to spare.[1]

Not all Eurocentric deviations, if *Ostpolitik* is resurrected, can now be headed off. But an EEC composed of Six rather than Ten or more would do most to keep them within bounds. The British people are often exhorted to enter the EEC for political reasons. By proposing a multilateral free trade area, one that

---

[1] On this point see the writer's article "Peaceful Coexistence or a Durable Peace?" *Orbis* (University of Pennsylvania), Summer, 1964, pp. 316-31.
Also Lionel Gelber *The Alliance of Necessity*, pp. 133-58 and in *New Trade Strategy for the World Economy* (ed. H. G. Johnson), pp. 114-18.

Britain might join instead, the United States could also convert an economic venture into an instrument of world politics. Only half the job is done when Washington examines the impact of the EEC from an economic standpoint. Whatever enlarges it might enlarge the zone of trade discrimination. The hazards that lurk in its enlargement, from a politico-strategic angle, would be no less acute.

Why, then, has the United States taken no countervailing initiative as yet? After doing so much to cultivate the EEC, she still detects in its enlargement little to disturb American primacy. But even if alarm bells had rung, proposals for trade liberalisation might not get far. In the Congress there has been a recrudescence of protectionist sentiment, some of it rekindled by EEC policies, some by the one-sided way in which Japan handles exports, imports and foreign investment. American trade unions have advocated trade liberalisation. They stopped doing so as, during the recent business recession, unemployment grew. Early in 1971, nevertheless, there was (with President Nixon's annual report to the Congress on foreign affairs) an appeal from Washington for a dismantling of those trade barriers to which the United States also resorts. Though this was addressed to Tokyo as well as Brussels, the European Community, enlarged or unenlarged, can give no satisfactory answer without putting itself into reverse. And that it is neither willing nor able to do.

Britain will thus have no adequate alternative in the offing when she has to make up her mind on this paramount issue. If she stays out of the EEC, lesser applicants may have to choose between their privileges in the British market and those that Brussels could supply. Some of them may depart from EFTA (the European Free Trade Association). More important than what happens is what does not happen. If Britain refrains from entry into the EEC any smaller Third Force, should one crystallise, would be that much less capable of making a stir. By the same token, though, it would not be as urgent for the United States to forestall, through a countervailing trade initiative, grave damage which the EEC might inflict upon the unity of the West.

Under these circumstances Britain could only preserve the *status quo* while exploring its possibilities with more assiduity. Another stage in the Kennedy Round begins in 1972 and so the EEC will be lowering tariff walls against British goods anyhow. Upon abstention from the Common Market, Britain would have forgone whatever economies of scale it might have bestown. It, nevertheless, should be no handicap for her as an exporter if she can still import low-cost foodstuffs from Commonwealth countries and still procure in them preferred treatment for her goods. Britain will have to phase out Commonwealth economic arrangements such as these if free trade is adopted; they will help tide her over until that day dawns. Nothing would go more against the grain than for her to become a mere extension of Continental land-power. It is through overseas affinities that she has lived, moved and had her being. Voluntary co-operation in every type of external endeavour will be better for her than the involuntary Eurocentric co-operation by which, on being Europeanised, she would be pinned down inexorably. Such factors as the Commonwealth or Anglo-American friendship now count for less than they once did. But saving remnants could, when necessary, still be reactivated.

It is too soon, moreover, to rule out the advent of a multilateral free trade area, one that might also do away with non-tariff trade barriers while temperate-zone agriculture is tackled as well. And if Washington should ever sponsor a scheme of this sort, there would still be those European countries that were anxious to enter the Common Market but, taking their cue from London, reluctantly backed down. Britain will not only have kept her own options open. She will have done the same for the United States.

And that being so, on what grounds would Washington entertain the idea of some wide-ranging project for the further liberalisation of world trade? It will be as well to forget that the British, if they steer clear, may have precluded an enlargement of the EEC that could weaken the power structure of the West. Gratitude in human affairs is the most transient of emotions. Britain may even be censured, if she fails to take the plunge, for having done the United States a good turn. The American interest, as defined in concrete terms against which sectional interests may still rebel, is what the incentive for a new American trade initiative will have to be.

It is patent that cheaper imports would pour balm into the lot of so many Americans with incomes at the mercy of a welfare state geared for inflation. At the same time the demand of American export industries, with agriculture among them, must always be for tariffs through which foreign customers can export to the United States in return. These, moreover, are items upon which Nixon Republicans and many Democrats have laid stress. Action could ensue. And if it does, political ends, some with an Anglo-American content, may again be served by economic means.

Trade is not the most glamorous of subjects and yet a new American initiative in this sphere could also do something to restore a sense of mission with which the United States has often been imbued. She may shun fresh military liabilities abroad and preoccupy herself with reconstruction at home. Beyond Western Europe, nevertheless, lies much that is alive and dynamic in the West. If the EEC is not enlarged, the United States is the one that can do most towards harnessing such energies for the well-being of mankind. No role short of leadership will hold antagonists at bay and the condition of American primacy, in the domain of trade as well as defence, is that the United States constantly take the lead. Between the furtherance of free trade and the progress of the free world it is not wholly fanciful to perceive a correlation.[1]

There is no room here to spell out other benefits in detail. Except for Ireland, applicants for entry into the Common Market are signatories of the North Atlantic Alliance. But that is not the sort of company with which European neutrals should be aligned or to which neutrals, dwelling in the shadow of the Soviet treaty, imperium, can belong, as Moscow has made evident, with impunity. Adherence to a multilateral free trade treaty, as adherence to EFTA has illustrated, would not invite the same trouble.

[1] For early criticism of the Europeanisation of Britain, see Lionel Gelber, *The American Anarchy*, New York 1953, pp. 180-81 and *America in Britain's Place*, New York and London 1961, pp. 147-51.

Arguments for a loose connection of Britain with the Common Market appeared in the writer's contribution to *The Statist*, London, March 9th, 1962.

For advocacy of a countervailing American initiative, see the text of a talk by the writer to a parliamentary group in the House of Commons published in the "Monthly Bulletin", Commonwealth Industries Association, London, December 1962.

For dissent from the celebrated Kennedy proposals for an Atlantic partnership, see Lionel Gelber, "A Marriage of Inconvenience", *Foreign Affairs*, New York, January 1963, pp. 320-22. See also Orbis, Summer 1963; an article by the writer in *Worldview*, New York, May 1964; and, more fully, *The Alliance of Necessity*.

For advocacy of a multilateral free trade area, see "World Politics and Trade Strategy" in *New Trade Strategy for the World Economy*. Also articles by the writer in *Worldview*, New York, June 1970 and *The New Statesman*, London, December 18th, 1970.

What has always been a non-starter is the notion that even the Common Market as a single entity, could join a multilateral free trade area. Its Common External Tariff is what cements it together and, until it abolishes this, it would be ineligible for membership. It cannot join as a single entity if it ceases to be a single entity on joining. But a multilateral free trade treaty might enable industrial countries to do more together than they are doing for those that hover on the threshold of development. A rich man's club, aware of its responsibilities, would, in that respect, be better for the poor than no club at all.

One hurdle is the outlook of Japan. It would be a long jump from her restrictive trade practices to trade liberalisation on a multilateral scale. If, however, a free trade area is formed without her, she might reply to such a grouping by moving closer to China and Russia—even though it is against them that the United States guarantees her defence. Rather than let that occur, with its unsettling effect on the security of the Western Pacific and South-East Asia, Washington itself may be loth to proceed. But as Japan climbs industrially and technologically, her own vistas must broaden. On the theme of aid and assistance she has a regional duty towards those less affluent than herself. Yet much in her own good fortune can be traced back to a free world order that the West upholds. The greater her stake in it, the more she must associate herself with those on whose shoulders its chief burdens rest. And if she does, Australia and New Zealand could both profit. Japan is already Australia's major trading partner while the United States is a major market for Japan, Australia and New Zealand. The United States underwrites the defence of these three countries. A trade ensemble that included all of them would be part of a still wider one which, by its sheer economic preponderance, could set standards for trade liberalisation to which most of the free world might rally.

Britain's decision thus affects more than Britain. And yet if she joined a multilateral free trade area, would she have evaded an organic merger with European neighbours only to be devoured economically, from across the Atlantic, by the mightiest of political unions? Whatever she does presents difficulties. Free trade might overwhelm her without faster growth and yet cost inflation must also be kept in check. Upon Britain's entry into the EEC, sheltered British industries would have had to brace themselves against competition from West Germany, France,

Italy, Belgium and the Netherlands. A treaty for multilateral free trade could similarly be rejected as a sluice-gate for a flood of American imports. British exporters and investors, however, would enjoy compensating opportunities within so lucrative an overseas market as the American—together with other remunerative ones in Europe and elsewhere. Not even Japan could get without also giving.

There is, too, something for Britain to garner from Canada's experience. As a North American nation, that country is more Americanised than Britain ever could be. She has, all the same, been staunch in preserving her national identity against the United States while, if Britain were to be Europeanised, encroachments upon British autonomy would be irresistible. As much as economic conquest from below the border, Canada is imperilled by disunity from within—not only by separatism in Quebec but by discontent on the Western prairies and on the Pacific seaboard. The Canadian electorate, as a matter of fact, voted against hemispheric reciprocity in bilateral trade with the United States as long ago as 1911. Today, however, the sheer diversity of a multilateral free trade area should make it safe. And if Japan also entered, it would, from the standpoint of exports, imports as well as foreign investment, be competitively even more diverse.

For the cause of free trade, then, this is a turning-point. The Europeanisation of Britain would stifle any American trade initiative prior to birth. If Britain ratifies the Treaty of Rome, Brussels will have most of non-Soviet Europe knocking on its door and the industrial countries with whom the United States could sign a free trade agreement are the very ones—Canada, Australia (with New Zealand again caught in a painful dilemma)—that must want the more rational trading equilibrium which a world-wide trade grouping might provide. That self-fulfilling prophecy of the Europeanisers, a world economy partitioned between semi-closed trade blocs, would be at hand. Internally, these monsters may digest those that enlarge them at a slow pace. The external havoc might be visible far sooner.

A new, non-isolationist type of Fortress America could match whatever drives the United States in upon herself. The result might be mounting American pressure upon Canada and Australia while, despite alliances, Washington tends to go it alone. Nor would there be a multilateral free trade area to beckon Japan more than ever towards the comity of the West. What might most attract the Japanese, though the United States still guarantees their security, is the Asian mainland. As for the future of less industrialised countries, their woes would not be allayed by trade bloc contests within the free world. Among developing countries, moreover, ill-will engendered between trade blocs of the non-Communist world may only expedite inroads by the adversaries of the West.

A turning-point in the world economy could thus also be one in world politics. What a multilateral free trade area might accomplish, if there is no enlargement of the EEC, is plain. It could well revive and lend itself to world-wide unities in one vital sphere without demolishing others of a politico-strategic character that are at least as vital. If Britain let herself become a mere outer island province of Continental land-power, she would have relinquished in peace what, for centuries, she would never surrender in war. Far better for her to adapt her economy to a code of more liberalised international trade in which she could still function as the centre of an oceanic system. Even a modest one would have the merit of allowing her to be herself again. A fully Europeanised role for Britain is what will do most to break up the Commonwealth, a great experiment with a value that outweighs its deficiencies. By the same token, unless Britain is the centre of an oceanic system, Anglo-American friendship cannot be conserved. When President Nixon reaffirmed the special relationship in December 1970 he was referring to what, despite unexpiated divergences, has been Britain's ultimate solidarity with the United States. And that is an American asset which the absorption of Britain by the EEC cannot liquidate, as it will, without putting the entire Atlantic nexus under strain.

Isolationism in the United States and appeasement in Britain fed each other between the wars. For an English-speaking élite again to misjudge basic issues is more than the West can afford. The latest fallacy to haunt British politicians and opinion-makers, Left, Right and Centre, was that, with less onerous terms, Britain could join the Common Market tolerably unscathed. She could not. The brute facts have been quite different and all she needed to know about them has long been known. What had to be warded off were threats to an independent role for Britain and to the unity of the West. It was not by striking a bargain at Brussels that these basic issues could be settled. The cost of admission was the most that the negotiations could ever determine. But entry into the hall itself would have been self-defeating at any price. The British people should not have paid to play a part in a perennial drama for which they would have been tragically unsuited.

Britain held the casting vote before the wars of 1914 and 1939 when a European balance of power had to be maintained. There would be no free world order today if the United States did not maintain a global balance. An erosion within the Western segment of that global balance is what Britain must now avert. She will be casting her vote erroneously if she prefers her own Europeanisation to the *status quo* and does not bide her time until something genuinely better than the *status quo* becomes feasible.

Much would be foreclosed by the enlargement and unification of the EEC. More full of promise for the rich and poor of the non-Soviet world is that liberalisation of trade between other industrial countries which a multilateral free trade treaty might foster. Only the United States, together with Britain and Canada, can bring it about. And if she does thus reassert herself in her own national interest, she could simultaneously offer the British people renewed hope and scope.